An In-depth Look at the
Defining Moments
of Christ's Passion

RICK RENNER

TEACH ALL NATIONS

A book company anointed to take God's Word
to you and to the nations of the world.

a division of
RICK RENNER MINISTRIES

Paid in Full:
An In-Depth Look at the Defining Moments of Christ's Passion
ISBN 978-0-9779459-1-7
Copyright © 2008 by Teach All Nations
P. O. Box 702040
Tulsa, OK 74170-2040

Editorial Consultants: Cynthia D. Hansen and Andrell Corbin
Text Design: Lisa Simpson and Diane Whisner
Graphic Design: Debbie Pullman, Zoe Life Creative Media
  Design@ZoeLifeCreative.com

Dedication

Every Sunday as I was growing up, my pastor, Rev. Robert Post, faithfully preached the Gospel of Jesus Christ. Each week with great conviction, compassion, and boldness, he unflinchingly proclaimed the death, burial, and resurrection of Jesus. His no-nonsense, unapologetic, clear-cut, compelling, and persuasive presentation of the Gospel dramatically affected me at a young age and still has a formidable influence on my thinking and my philosophy of ministry today.

In this day and age, the preaching of the Cross has become more and more of a rare occurrence. It makes me want to pause and thank God that I had a pastor who faithfully drove the truth of the Cross into my heart, helping me to cherish the Cross and to value the great price that Jesus was willing to pay for me. Over the 20 years Brother Post ministered at our church, his commitment to preach this most important message the world has ever heard never wavered. As a result, I saw many people genuinely repent and come to a saving knowledge of Jesus Christ at the altar of our church.

Today it's been nearly 50 years since I first sat under the ministry of my pastor. For decades, I, too, have been giving altar calls and have seen thousands of people commit their lives to Jesus Christ. I would be remiss if I didn't stop to say *thank you* to this precious man for teaching me that leading a soul to Christ is the most important and eternal act I can ever do.

As I stand in front of my own congregation and before audiences in meetings around the world, it is now *my* responsibility to call sinners to repentance and the backslidden to recommitment. As I do, I often remember Brother Post standing before me and the rest of the church, giving his own altar calls. I can still hear his voice as he walked the aisles and passionately begged people to make their hearts right with God.

Brother Post, there is no doubt that today, at least in part, I mirror the example you lived before me as I grew up in your church. I want to dedicate this book to you, for God mightily used you to drive the message of the Cross deep into my heart. Thank you for demonstrating compassionate love for the lost and for teaching me that leading a soul to Christ is the greatest honor in the world. This was, is, and always will be the greatest and most important message I could ever preach.

My dear pastor, I know that when we all stand before Jesus, much of what has been accomplished through my life and ministry will be accredited to your account, for you have been so instrumental in helping to form who I am and what I believe today. So much of the passion in my heart and the work God is doing through my life is a result of what you imparted to me through your faithful years of service. Thank you from the bottom of my heart.

Rick Renner

Table of Contents

Acknowledgments 7

Introduction 9

1   Jesus' Final Words 11

2   Wounds of Betrayal 19

3   Agony of the Soul 25

4   Divine Assistance 31

5   How Many Soldiers Does It Take To Arrest One Man? 37

6   Misunderstandings and Suspicions 45

7   Kiss of Deception 53

8   Test of Loyalty, Test of Love 61

9   Paralyzed by His Presence 69

10   The Danger of Taking Matters Into Your Own Hands 75

11   Jesus Cleans Up Peter's Mess! 83

12   Twelve Legions of Angels 89

13   Who Was the Naked Boy in the Garden of Gethsemane? 95

14   A Holy Life Laid Down for You .101

15   Has Anyone Ever Spit in Your Face? 109

16   Playing Games at Jesus' Expense 117

17   Surrender and Release Yourself
      Into the Loving Care of God 125

18   Pilate Looks for a Loophole! 135

19   Herod Meets Jesus! 143

20   A Human Ruler Mocks the King of Kings
       and Lord of Lords 153

21   Charged, but Not Guilty 161

22   The Horror of a Roman Scourging 169

23   Tortured for You 177

24   Golgotha: The Place of the Skull 187

25   Crucified! 193

26   It Is Finished! 203

27   The Day the Earth Trembled 213

28   A Burial of Love 219

29   Buried and Sealed 229

30   Behold, He Is Risen! 239

31   An Empty Tomb 249

32   The First Woman Preacher 257

33   Eyewitness Accounts That Jesus Rose From the Dead 265

34   What Has Jesus Been Doing for the Past 2,000 Years? 275

35   Copy Every Stroke of the Master 287

Isn't It Time To Make a Change in Your Life? 297
     Prayer of Salvation 301
     Prayer of Forgiveness 303
     Prayer for Healing 305

Acknowledgments

I would like to thank the people who participated in this book project: Matt Jones, who conducted research and provided needed documentation; Jeremy Rhodes, who oversaw the physical printing of this book; graphic artist Debbie Pullman, who designed the cover; and editors Andrell Corbin and Cindy Hansen for their wonderful editorial contributions and suggestions. God has blessed Denise and me with a fabulous team, and we are thankful to each member for his or her contribution. Specifically, I am grateful to these five team members for their part in the production of this long-awaited book.

Rick Renner

Introduction

Easter was always a big day in our home, as it is in most Christian homes. The day on which we celebrate may not be the actual day the event took place, but it is nonetheless a special day to remember and celebrate Jesus' victory over sin, death, and the grave. *It is a sanctified time to focus on the price paid for our souls.* How I thank God that Easter was celebrated by my parents and by the church we attended. It's a memory I'll always cherish!

Unfortunately, far too often we never even think about the final days of Jesus' life except at Easter time. Although the final days of Jesus' life are filled with truths and principles to guide our lives, we don't stop to consider the profound significance of all that happened to Him during that time.

But everything about this story — *everything* — is relevant and applicable to your everyday life. This powerful, life-changing story should not be relegated to one day a year when you celebrate Easter. *This is the story of all stories, filled with truths and pertinent principles that will empower you to overcome in every area of your life!* So I urge you to open your heart as you read the truths contained in these pages. Study to see what you can learn from Jesus to help you walk as He walked on this earth.

It is my prayer that by the time you reach the end of this book, you will have gained a far deeper understanding of the price Jesus paid to set you free — and that as a result, you will never be the same.

Rick Renner
Moscow, Russia
November 1, 2007

chapter

1

Jesus' Final Words

chapter

1

Jesus' Final Words

On the night when Jesus was betrayed, He got on His knees and washed His disciples' feet. Then He served the disciples their first Communion as He confirmed His covenant with them. Afterward, Jesus began to speak the *last words* He would ever speak to them in His human form, before He received a glorified body. As Jesus looked into the eyes of His disciples, He knew this was the last time He'd speak to them in this capacity. He also knew that these last words would be among the most important words He had *ever* spoken to them.

So what did Jesus say to His disciples in those final, intimate moments with them?

Think about what *you* would talk about if you knew you were looking into the eyes of your family members and friends for the last time. I seriously doubt you'd joke or make a lot of small talk.

Such moments are hallowed and sacred. It would be a time for you to carefully weigh your words and to speak what you believe is most important for your listeners to remember after you are gone.

- ❖ If you had the opportunity to speak your *last* words to those you love, wouldn't you carefully choose the words you spoke in that final moment?

- ❖ Wouldn't it be a time to say the things that were most important and dear to your heart — words that communicated the deepest feelings of your soul to your loved ones?

If you are like the majority of other human beings, it would be your greatest desire in that final moment to make your last words the most thoughtful, advantageous, and heartfelt words you could leave with the people who mean the most to you.

In every person's life, there are key moments when he or she is faced with the need to speak *concluding words*.

❖ Before a person slips into eternity, he often prays for an opportunity to speak final words of farewell to his loved ones.

❖ A person may need to speak final words at his workplace because of a job change that requires him to relocate and thereby leave behind associates and friends with whom he has worked for a long time.

❖ Parents come to that moment when they must carefully speak their last words to their son or daughter right before their child stands before a minister and commits his or her life to someone else in marriage.

There are many different reasons you might need to speak *last words* at various times in your life. Can you think of a time in particular when you had to choose final words to speak to people whom you deeply loved?

I remember such a moment in my life. After serving one church for many years and literally pouring our hearts and souls into that congregation, Denise and I sensed that it was time for us to follow God's call elsewhere. The days passed and the time drew nearer to our last church service with our congregation. More and more I became aware that when I stood before the people as senior pastor for the last time, I'd be preaching the most important message I'd ever preached to that church.

In the years we had served in this church, the congregation had heard many of my sermons. But in that last service, I'd be speaking my *last words* to them as their senior pastor. Therefore, I knew my words had to be carefully chosen and sensitively spoken. It was essential that I leave them with the message that was most important for them to hear from me as I stood before them for the last time in the role of their senior pastor.

After Jesus washed His disciples' feet and served them their first Communion, He stayed with them and taught them for a lengthy period of time. We don't know exactly how long Jesus' teaching lasted that night, but three entire chapters (John 14, 15, and 16) are devoted to His last words to His disciples. These chapters contain the Spirit-inspired record of what Jesus said to His disciples just hours before He went to the Cross and the grave. This would be the last time He'd ever speak to them as the Leader they had known in human form.

Jesus was about to physically depart from this world. He knew it was absolutely essential that the disciples learn how to rely entirely on the Spirit of God for guidance and direction after He left. Therefore, Jesus used His last moments to teach the disciples how to follow the Holy Spirit's leadership in the same way they had followed Him.

It must have seemed strange to the disciples as they listened to Jesus speak about the Holy Spirit. They had been accustomed to Jesus physically and visibly leading them, but now they were learning that the Spirit of God would become their Leader. This would be a Leader they couldn't see, couldn't touch, and couldn't audibly hear; yet they were supposed to follow Him just as they had followed Jesus. They were probably thinking, *What is the Holy Spirit's leadership going to be like in our lives? Does He act and think differently than Jesus? What is it going to be like to follow the Spirit of God?*

Knowing that these were normal questions to ask, Jesus used His final moments with the disciples to dispel all fear and insecurity they might have felt about following the Holy Spirit's leadership. This is why Jesus was so careful to use key words when He spoke to them about the coming of the Holy Spirit. In John 14:16, for example, Jesus said, "And I will pray the Father, and he shall give you another Comforter...."

I want to draw your attention to a very important word in this verse — the word "another." In Greek, there are two possible words for "another." The first is the Greek word *allos*, and the second is the Greek word *heteros*. The word *allos* means *one of the very same kind*; *same character*; *same everything*; or *nearly a duplicate*. The second word, *heteros*, means *one of another kind* or *one of a different kind*. This word *heteros* forms the first part of the word *heterosexual*, which, of course, describes someone who has sexual relations with a person of the opposite sex.

Jesus used His final moments with the disciples to dispel all fear and insecurity they might have felt about following the Holy Spirit's leadership.

The Greek word used in John 14:16 is the first word, *allos*. The word *allos* emphatically means that *the Holy Spirit would be like Jesus in every way*. This conveys a very strong and important message about the Holy Spirit. Jesus wanted the disciples to know that the Holy Spirit was just like Him. Following the Holy Spirit wouldn't be any different than following Him, except the Spirit's leadership would be invisible rather than physical and visible, as Jesus' leadership had been.

John 14:16 could thus be translated to mean: *"I will pray the Father, and He will send you Someone who is just like Me in every way. He will be identical to Me in the way He speaks, the way He thinks, the way He operates, the way He see things, and the way He does things. He will be exactly like Me in every way. If the Holy Spirit is here, it will be just as if I am here because We think, behave, and operate exactly the same."*

Earlier in John 14, Philip told the Lord, "…Shew us the Father, and it sufficeth us" (John 14:8). Jesus answered, "…Have I been so long time with you, and yet hast thou not known me, Philip? he that hath seen me hath seen the Father; and how sayest thou then, Shew us the Father" (John 14:9).

Jesus was the exact image of the Father when He walked on this earth. Hebrews 1:3 (*AMP*) declares, "He is the sole expression of the glory of God [the Light-being, the out-raying or radiance of the divine], and He is the perfect imprint and very image of [God's] nature...." This means Jesus reflected the character of His Heavenly Father in every way. That is why Jesus told Philip, "...He that hath seen me hath seen the Father...."

Although the Father, Son, and Holy Spirit are each distinct Members of the Godhead, there is only one God, and each Person of the Godhead shares the same substance and essence. So if you see Jesus, you see the Father. By looking at Jesus, you can discover the Father's will. Jesus did and said exactly what the Father would do and say. His life, attitudes, and actions were the absolute manifested will of the Father, for the two were united in nature, in character, in thought, and in deed.

As Jesus teaches the disciples about the Holy Spirit, He takes this truth one step further. Just as Jesus is the exact image of the Father in every way, now Jesus unmistakably tells the disciples that when the Holy Spirit comes, He will exactly represent Jesus in every word. That's why the word *allos* is used to make this point. It leaves no room for doubt that the Holy Spirit will be exactly like Jesus.

The word *allos* tells us the Holy Spirit perfectly represents the life and nature of Jesus Christ. Jesus did only what the Heavenly Father would do, and now the Holy Spirit will do only what Jesus would do. As Jesus' Representative on earth, the Holy Spirit never acts on His own or out of character with the life of Jesus Christ.

You see, the Spirit of God was sent to bring us the life of Jesus. Just as Jesus told Philip, "If you've seen Me, you've seen the Father," now He is telling us, "If you have the Holy Spirit, it will be just as if you have Me."

I've often heard Christians ask, "I wonder what it must have been like to walk with Jesus. Wouldn't it be wonderful to walk with Him and to hear His voice and talk to Him?" But believers who ask these kinds of questions don't understand the ministry of the Holy Spirit. If they did, they'd know that having the Holy Spirit with them is just like having Jesus right at their side!

You and I must stop looking backward and grieving over what we missed by not living 2,000 years ago. Instead, we must learn to let the Holy Spirit lead and guide us, just as He did in the Early Church. Jesus' physical absence didn't stop the early believers from performing miracles, raising the dead, casting out demons, healing the sick, or bringing multitudes to a saving knowledge of Jesus Christ. Because the Holy Spirit was with them, the ministry of Jesus continued uninterrupted in their midst.

Never forget — as a child of God, you have the Holy Spirit working within you and alongside you every moment of every day. And because the Holy Spirit is the exact representation of your Lord and Savior, it's just like having Jesus right there at your side.

Jesus' last words to His disciples revolved around the ministry of the Holy Spirit in the lives of believers. That's how serious this message was to Jesus! Since Jesus considered this subject to be so important, why don't you open your heart to the work of the Spirit today? Let the Holy Spirit represent Jesus to you, your church, your family, your business, and your city, just as He did to believers who lived during the time of the book of Acts.

Think About It

Your last words to a person, or your final words on a matter, establish a defining moment. Whatever may have transpired before, or whatever may follow afterward, is to be understood and viewed through the lens of those concluding words.

As you consider Jesus' final words to His disciples, think about those individuals for whom you care deeply. If you knew you were slipping into eternity or permanently changing locations, what would your words be to them, and why?

Jesus gave an in-depth description of the Holy Spirit to His disciples. He even told them it was to their advantage that He was going away, for then the Holy Spirit could come into their lives. Unlike Jesus, who at that time could only be *with* them, the Person of the Holy Spirit would move among Jesus' followers collectively and dwell within them individually.

Imagine a scenario in your life in light of this knowledge that you have that kind of supernatural help to you. What distinct advantages open up to you as a result of having constant access to a wise Counselor who is willing to help you in every conceivable way and to give you the right solution to every possible situation?

In what specific ways are you pursuing a deeper relationship with the Person of the Holy Spirit?

chapter

2

Wounds of Betrayal

chapter

2

Wounds of Betrayal

Have you ever felt betrayed by a friend or by someone you dearly loved? When it happened, were you *shocked*? Did it feel like that person put a knife in your back by violating your trust and revealing things that should have been kept in confidence? Did you marvel that such a trusted friend could turn out to be so disloyal? Did you wonder, *How in the world could a person so dear and close be used so viciously by the devil to attack me in this way?*

It's painful when a friend betrays you. It's even worse when the person is your best friend or someone you've known and trusted for many years.

Betrayal is something that has happened to people since the beginning of time. It is simply a fact that the devil is a master at distorting and ruining relationships. He knows how to lure people into situations where they end up feeling offended or hurt; then he coaxes them into nurturing their offense until it mutates into strife that separates even the best of friends and the closest family members.

Don't forget — Satan was kicked out of Heaven because of his unique ability to create confusion, discord, and strife. Heaven is as perfect as an environment can be. Yet in that perfect environment, the devil was still able to affect one-third of the angels with his slanderous allegations against God. Angels who had worshiped together for eons of time now stood opposed to each other over issues the devil had conjured up in their minds.

That should tell you how clever the devil is at creating discord and strife! If the devil is persuasive enough to do this with angels, think how much easier it is for him to deceive people who live in a far-from-perfect environment and who wrestle daily with their own imperfections and self-image!

Satan watches for that opportune moment when a person is tired, weary, or exasperated. Then he waits until someone does something that person doesn't understand or agree with. Suddenly it is as if the devil shoots a fiery arrow of rage straight into the person's emotions! Before long, strife, bitterness, unforgiveness, and division begin to mount. Friends who once stood side by side and cherished each other now stand facing each other as hostile rivals.

If this sounds familiar, be encouraged! This same scenario happened to *Jesus*! After working with Judas Iscariot for three years, the devil found his way into Judas' soul, turning him so sour against Jesus that this disciple became His betrayer.

But we need to ask: *What opened the door for this deception to occur inside Judas?*

In John 13:2, the Bible gives us a very powerful insight into the way the devil establishes a foothold in people's minds. Back in John 12:3-7, Mary brought a pound of spikenard and poured it on Jesus' feet. Judas thought her act of love was a waste of money and took issue with Jesus about it. But Jesus told Judas to leave Mary alone and allowed her to continue. John 13:2 then tells us, "And supper being ended, the devil having now put into the heart of Judas Iscariot, Simon's son, to betray him."

What was the exact moment that Satan put this thought into Judas' heart? Apparently, it was when Judas became offended with Jesus about the spikenard. Perhaps Judas didn't agree with Jesus' decision, or maybe he didn't like the fact that Jesus told him to leave Mary alone. Or maybe it was because Judas was a thief. As the ministry treasurer who stole regularly from the moneybag he held, he probably didn't like it when money was spent elsewhere instead of being placed in the treasury!

Whatever the reason, it was at that moment of disagreement that the devil found an open door into Judas' heart.

Especially notice the phrase "...the devil having now put into the heart of Judas Iscariot...." The words "put into" come from the Greek word *ballo*, which means *to throw*, *to cast*, *to thrust*, or *to inject*. This word *ballo* carries the idea of *a very fast action of throwing, thrusting, or injecting something forward*, such as the throwing of a ball or rock, or the forward thrusting of a sharp knife.

It is significant that this word was used in this context, because it tells us how quickly the devil moved to inject a seed of betrayal into Judas' heart. When the seed of betrayal was injected, it went so deep that it turned Judas — one of Jesus' closest associates — into a deceiver and a betrayer. Judas became the epitome of a disloyal and unfaithful friend.

When Satan finally penetrated Judas' mind and emotions with this seed of betrayal, he injected it so hard and fast that it became *deeply embedded* or *lodged* in Judas' soul.

John 13:2 could therefore be translated:*"...the devil having now thrust into...."*; *"...the devil having now inserted into...."*; *"...the devil having now forcibly hurled into...."*; or *"...the devil having now embedded into...."*

There is no doubt that the word *ballo* means the devil *quickly seized* an opportunity *to inject* a seed of betrayal into Judas' heart. He was so offended by Jesus that a window to his heart and emotions opened, even if only for a brief moment. When the devil saw that opening, he moved like lightning to penetrate Judas' mind and emotions in order to sour a long-term relationship and turn a trusted friend into a betrayer.

Satan was able to use Judas as his instrument because Judas allowed the enemy to drive a wedge between him and Jesus. Rather than let go of the disagreement and forget about it, Judas let the issue become a big deal in his mind — something so blown out of proportion that the devil was able to use the offense to lure him into the ultimate act of disloyalty. Because Judas didn't take his thoughts captive, the devil succeeded in tainting his view of Jesus. This then led to a disastrous effect on Judas' relationship with Him.

It is important that you learn how to recognize those times when the devil tries to inject a seed of division into your heart. He wants to drive a wedge between you and the people you love. Rather than let him get away with this evil tactic, make a decision to resist every temptation to get angry and offended. By resisting these thoughts, you can take a stand against the devil and protect your relationships.

Learn how to recognize those times when the devil tries to inject a seed of division into your heart. He wants to drive a wedge between you and the people you love.

Learn from the example of Judas Iscariot. Determine that you will never let any issue get so blown out of proportion that it turns you into a disloyal, lying, betraying friend. And if you are hurting right now because someone has recently betrayed and hurt you, *choose the route of forgiveness*. Remember, what you sow is what you reap — and if you sow forgiveness now, you will reap forgiveness from others when you need it in the future.

Think About It

The devil is a destroyer and is therefore masterful when it comes to ruining relationships. Can you recall a time in your own life when the devil used a friend or someone you trusted to betray you, violate your trust, or cause you grief and inward pain? What are the lessons you learned as a result of walking with God through such a difficult experience?

Has there ever been a time when the devil used you to betray someone else? Did you ever stop to think of the pain you brought into that person's life as a result of your actions? Did you ever go back to him or her to ask for forgiveness and to try to make it right?

Relationships are a vital element in the fabric of our lives. People can use their influence in our lives either to aid or to hinder our divine purpose. Think of some of the crucial relationships in your life. In what way can you add value to those individuals' lives to strengthen them along the course of their divine destiny?

chapter

3

Agony of the Soul

chapter

3

Agony of the Soul

Have you ever wondered where all your friends were at a time when you really needed them? Perhaps they pledged they would be faithful, but when you needed those friends most, they were nowhere to be found. Did you feel abandoned in that moment of need?

Jesus Himself was confronted with that same situation when He was in the Garden of Gethsemane on the night before His crucifixion. After He was finished serving Communion to His disciples in the upper room, the Bible tells us that He went to the Garden of Gethsemane with them. Knowing that the Cross and the grave lay before Him, Jesus felt a need to spend time in intercession so He might gain the strength He needed to face what lay before Him. He also requested that Peter, James, and John come apart to pray with Him.

> *Knowing that the Cross and the grave lay before Him, Jesus felt a need to spend time in intercession so He might gain the strength He needed to face what lay before Him.*

Rarely, if ever, did Jesus need His friends' assistance. Most of the time, they needed His! But in this intense moment, Jesus really felt a need to have the three disciples who were closest to Him pray with Him. Jesus asked these disciples to pray for just one hour. But instead of faithfully praying when Jesus desperately needed their support, the three disciples kept falling asleep!

The mental and spiritual battle Jesus experienced that night in the Garden of Gethsemane was *intense*. In fact, Luke 22:44 says, "And being in an agony he prayed more earnestly: and his sweat was as it were great drops of blood falling down to the ground."

I want you to especially notice the word "agony" in this verse. It comes from the Greek word *agonidzo*, a word that refers to *a struggle, a fight, great exertion*, or *effort*. It is a word often used in the New Testament to convey the ideas of *anguish, pain, distress*, and *conflict*. The word *agonidzo* itself comes from the word *agon*, which is the word that depicted the *athletic conflicts and competitions* that were so famous in the ancient world.

The Holy Spirit used this word to picture Jesus in the Garden of Gethsemane on the night of His betrayal. This tells us that Jesus was thrown into *a great struggle* or an *intense fight* that night. Knowing that the Cross and the grave were before Him, He cried out, "Father, if thou be willing, remove this cup from me..." (Luke 22:42).

The spiritual pressure that bore down upon Jesus' soul was so overwhelming that the Bible says it was *agonidzo*, or *agony*. It was so strenuous that it involved all of Jesus' spirit, soul, and body. He was in the greatest fight He had ever known up to that moment.

Jesus' intense level of agony is depicted in the phrase, "...he prayed more *earnestly*...." The word "earnestly" is the Greek word *ektenes*, a Greek word that means *to be extended* or *to be stretched out*. A person in this kind of agony might drop to the ground, writhing in pain and rolling around on the ground. This word *ektenes* presents the picture of a person who is pushed to the limit and can't be stretched much more. He is on the brink of all he can possibly endure.

Jesus' emotional state was so intense that it says "...his sweat was as it were great drops of blood falling down to the ground." The "sweat" is the Greek word *idros*. The word "drops" is the Greek word *thrombos*, a medical word that points to *blood that is unusually thickly clotted*. When these two words are joined, they depict a medical condition called *hematidrosis* — a condition that occurs only in individuals who are in a highly emotional state.

Because the mind is under such great mental and emotional pressure, it sends signals of stress throughout the human body. These signals become so strong that the body reacts as if it were under actual physical pressure. As a result, the first and second layer of skin separate, causing a vacuum to form between them. Thickly clotted blood seeps from this vacuum, oozing through the pores of the skin. Once the blood seeps through, it mingles with the sufferer's sweat that pours from his skin as a result of his intense inner struggle. In the end, the blood and sweat mix together in droplets and flow down the victim's face to the ground.

This was the worst spiritual combat Jesus had ever endured up to this time. And where were His disciples when He needed them? They were *sleeping*! Jesus needed His closest friends — yet they couldn't even pray for one hour! So God provided strength for Him in another way, which we will see in the next chapter.

Have you ever felt a need for help but found your friends couldn't be counted on? Did you find your friends sleeping on the job when you felt a deep need for help and support? Were you in a situation that caused you to feel intense agony and that pushed you to the limit? Are you in that kind of situation right now?

Maybe you've never sweat blood, but more than likely, you have struggled in your soul at one time or another because of problems with your marriage, your children, your relationships, your ministry, or your finances. If you've ever felt like you were constantly living in a "pressure cooker," you know that continuous pressure is hard to deal with — *especially* if you have no one to lean on for strength, encouragement, and help.

If you are experiencing one of those times right now, Jesus understands because He faced the same situation in the Garden of

Gethsemane. Hebrews 2:18 says, "For in that he himself hath suffered being tempted, he is able to succour them that are tempted." Because of what Jesus experienced, He is able to understand everything you are thinking and feeling.

I encourage you to set aside a few minutes to pray before you take one more step or make one more decision today. Talk to Jesus about the situations you are facing. He empathizes completely, and He will give you the strength you need to come through every one of life's "pressure cookers" victoriously.

Think About It

Intense emotional stress produces mental and physical distress. Jesus not only suffered on every level, He persevered through pain more difficult than you can conceive. Therefore, He not only completely understands everything you could possibly go through, He even empathizes with you. Have you ever thought about that before?

Jesus experienced the full range of human emotion and emotional strain. He knows exactly what it's like to feel pressure bearing down on Him from every side. Because Jesus understands stress, He can be trusted to understand and to help you no matter what you may be facing. What are the areas in your life where you are experiencing stress? Invite Jesus into that area and trust Him to help you. He will.

Sometimes it's easier to talk with someone who has already been through what you're experiencing. But do you still hurt after talking to your parents, your friends, your spouse, or your pastor? It's time for you to talk to Jesus. He is the Perfect One to talk to about your struggles because He understands better than anyone else.

chapter
4
Divine Assistance

chapter

4

Divine Assistance

I'll never forget the time years ago that our ministry was under a great assault. For no reason we could logically explain, the financial gifts of our partners seemed to dry up and dwindle away for a number of months. After this drought had gone on for quite a while, our situation became very serious. I didn't know how we were going to pay for our television broadcasts that covered the length and breadth of the former Soviet Union. It was time to pay the bills, and I didn't have the money.

As I walked through the city of Moscow on a cold winter night, I broke inside from the pressure I'd been feeling. I stopped at Red Square, leaned against a rail, and literally wept, not even caring about the people who passed by me. I felt so frustrated because I didn't know what to do. We had drained everything we had to keep those broadcasts on the air. Millions of people watched our television programs, and those hungry souls were depending on us. God had entrusted me with taking His Word to these former Soviet nations, and I took that responsibility seriously. But because our finances had dwindled, I found myself in an extremely hard spot.

After riding on the subway system for several hours while I tried to pull my thoughts together, I felt myself sinking deeper into a feeling of desperation. The reality was that if something didn't happen quickly to change the situation, I would have to cancel our program, and all those millions who waited for it each week would lose the teaching of God's Word.

I had just come up from the subway on my way to the television meeting when I leaned against that rail in Red Square and wept before the Lord. I felt so alone, so trapped, so unable to fix my problem. There didn't seem to be anyone I could call or turn to who could comprehend the enormity of what I was tackling in the spiritual realm that night.

I cried out, *"Lord, why has this happened? Is there a reason our supporters have temporarily stopped their support? Have we done anything that opened a door for the devil to disrupt our finances? Please tell me what I am supposed to do right now about this situation. What about the millions of people who are waiting for Your Word? Do we just disappear from television and leave them wondering what happened to us?"*

All of a sudden, it felt like a divine force entered me! Strength and courage flooded into my soul. I knew God was touching me, giving me a new supernatural boost of courage and faith to face this moment victoriously. Within minutes, my tears disappeared, my desperation vanished, and I began to celebrate the victory! Although I still didn't have the cash in hand to cover all the television bills, I knew the battle had been won in the Spirit. As it turned out, the money didn't come in all at once, but the valve had been turned on again and the gifts of our partners began to flow back into the ministry. I thank God for the supernatural assistance He gave me that night!

Have you ever known a time when you felt alone in the challenge you were facing? On the night of Jesus' betrayal, He must have felt that way. He asked His closest disciples — Peter, James, and John — to come apart and pray with Him in those last hours. But every time He came back to check on the three men, they were sleeping. As we've seen, Jesus was experiencing a great spiritual battle and extreme pressure that night. That's why He wanted His closest disciples to assist Him in prayer. However, that night they were not found faithful.

But when Jesus could find no one to stand with Him in His hour of need, God provided supernatural assistance! Luke 22:43 says, "And there appeared an angel unto him from heaven, strengthening him." This supernatural strength made up for any lack of support from His three closest disciples.

When Luke writes that the angel "strengthened" him, he uses the Greek word *enischuo*. This is a compound of the words *en* and *ischuos*. The word *en* means *in*, and the word *ischuos* is the word for *might* or *strength*. Normally in New Testament times, the word *ischuos* was used to denote *men with great muscular abilities*, similar to the bodybuilders in today's world. But when these two words *en* and *ischuos* are compounded together, the new word means *to impart strength*; *to empower someone*; *to fill a person with heartiness*; or *to give someone a renewed vitality*. A person may have been feeling exhausted and depleted, but he suddenly gets a blast of energy so robust that he is *instantly recharged*! Now he is ready to get up, get with it, and get going again!

This means that when Jesus' disciples and friends couldn't be depended on in His hour of need, God provided an angel that *empowered*, *recharged*, and *imparted strength to* Jesus, *renewing His vitality* with the strength needed to victoriously face the most difficult hour in His life. After being super-charged, Jesus was ready to face the Cross. He awakened His disciples and said, "Rise up, let us go; lo, he that betrayeth me is at hand" (Mark 14:42).

> *God is absolutely committed to seeing you through the situation you're facing. And, if necessary, He will provide supernatural assistance to recharge you and keep you moving full steam ahead.*

Maybe you've experienced a time in your life when *you* felt trapped and alone. Perhaps you thought your friends would help you, but then they let you down at a time when you really needed them.

If that scenario sounds all too familiar to you, don't let desperation take over! Your friends may have fallen asleep on the job, but God hasn't! He is absolutely committed to seeing you through the situation you're facing. And, if necessary, He will provide supernatural assistance to recharge you and keep you moving full steam ahead. You may be tempted to feel isolated and alone, but if the eyes of your spirit were opened for just a moment, you'd see that you're not alone at all! God is surrounding you with the Holy Spirit's power, with angels, and with anything else you need to keep going forward.

Regardless of the particular battle or situation you are facing in life, God will always come to your assistance. The same divine help He provided for Jesus in the Garden, He will provide for you. When no one else is faithful, you can rest assured that God is *always* faithful. He will see to it that you receive the strength and power you need to triumph in every circumstance.

Supernatural assistance is a part of your inheritance as a child of God. All you have to do to receive that assistance is claim it by faith and then walk in obedience to what God tells you to do.

Think About It

At times, circumstances arise in life when we feel utterly helpless. Remember a time in your life when you had neither the resources nor the ability to produce change in a certain situation, but God intervened to strengthen and energize you. God is the same today as He was yesterday. Remind yourself of His faithfulness, especially when you are tired and tempted to fear that you won't make it through a present challenge.

Think of a time when you felt trapped and alone. Perhaps your friends either could not or would not help you. Recount the ways God stepped in and proved to you that He neither slumbers nor sleeps. He has never abandoned you. If you appear to be alone in the midst of difficulty, always remember: *From the moment you call upon Him, God answers.*

If Jesus needed supernatural help, then you will need it! Think of a present situation in your life where you need divine intervention. Don't be ashamed to ask God for help. Simply turn to Him with your whole heart and declare, "I am Yours — save me!" Then allow God's power to strengthen you in the midst of that situation you are facing right now.

chapter

5

*How Many Soldiers
Does It Take To Arrest
One Man?*

chapter

5

How Many Soldiers Does It Take To Arrest One Man?

Jesus has the greatest power in the whole universe! During His earthly ministry, He healed the sick, cast out demons, raised the dead, walked on water, changed water into wine, and multiplied loaves and fishes. In fact, Jesus performed so many miracles that the apostle John said, "And there are also many other things which Jesus did, the which, if they should be written every one, I suppose that even the world itself could not contain the books that should be written..." (John 21:25).

Satan was terrified of Jesus. That's why the enemy inspired Herod the Great to try to kill the infant Messiah by slaughtering all the babies in Bethlehem and the surrounding region (Matthew 2:16). When that failed, the devil tried to wipe out Jesus by attempting to seduce Him with temptations in the wilderness. And when *that* failed, Satan tried to kill Jesus on numerous occasions using angry religious people!

Do you recall the many times religious leaders tried and failed to catch Jesus? The Gospels are filled with examples when He supernaturally slipped out of the hands of His aggressors. (*See* Luke 4:30, John 7:30, John 8:59, and John 10:39.)

After Jesus' last supper with His disciples, it was time for Satan's next attempt to destroy Jesus, this time using Judas Iscariot — and it seems that the devil was worried he wouldn't succeed again. Thus, the enemy inspired Judas to lead a massive group of Roman soldiers and temple police to arrest Jesus. There were far too many soldiers in this group to capture just one individual — *unless that individual was the Son of God*!

The religious leaders whom the devil was using were also filled with hate toward Jesus. Considering how many times Jesus had previously slipped out of their hands, they must have been worried that He might slip away this time as well.

After serving Communion to His disciples, Jesus retreated to the Garden of Gethsemane to pray. John 18:2 tells us that it was Jesus' custom to go there to pray with His disciples. Therefore, Judas knew precisely where to find Jesus that night when it was time to lead the soldiers and temple police to arrest Him.

John 18:3 says, "Judas then, having received a band of men and officers from the chief priests and Pharisees, cometh thither with lanterns and torches and weapons." This verse says Judas received "...a band of men and officers from the chief priests and Pharisees...." I want you to understand exactly who this "band of men" and these "officers from the chief priests" were so you can see the full picture of what happened that night on the Mount of Olives. I believe you will be flabbergasted when you realize the gigantic numbers of armed men who came looking for Jesus that night!

The soldiers Judas brought with him to the Garden of Gethsemane were soldiers who served at the Tower of Antonia — a tower that had been built by the Hasmonean rulers.[1] Later it was renamed the "Tower of Antonia" by King Herod in honor of one of his greatest patrons, Marc Antony (yes, the same Marc Antony who fell in love with the Egyptian queen Cleopatra!).

The Tower of Antonia was a massive edifice that was built on a rock and rose 75 feet into the air. Its sides had been completely smoothed flat to make it difficult for enemies to scale its walls. Although it had many towers, the highest one was located on the southeast corner, giving the watchman an uninhibited view of the temple area as well as much of Jerusalem.

Inside this massive complex was a large inner courtyard for exercising the Roman cohort — comprised of 300 to 600 specially trained soldiers — that was stationed there. These troops were poised to act defensively in the event of an insurgency or riot. In fact, a staircase led from the tower into the temple, enabling the troops to enter the temple in a matter of minutes should a disturbance develop there. One writer has noted that there was even a secret passageway from the tower to the inner court of the priests, making it possible for troops to reach even that holy, off-limits location.

John 18:3 records that there was "a band of men" in the Garden of Gethsemane that night. The Greek word for "a band of men" is *spira*. This is the word that describes *a military cohort* — the group of 300 to 600 soldiers mentioned above. These extremely well-trained soldiers were equipped with the finest weaponry of the day.

John 18:3 also tells us that on the night Jesus was arrested, this band of soldiers was accompanied by "officers from the chief priests and Pharisees." The word "officers" is from the Greek word *huperetas*. The word *huperetas* had several meanings in New Testament times, but in this case, it described the "police officers" who worked on the temple grounds. Once a judgment was given from the religious court of law, it was the responsibility of the temple police to execute these judgments. This fearsome armed force worked daily with the cohort stationed at the Tower of Antonia and reported to the chief priests, the Pharisees, and the Sanhedrin. These were the "officers" who accompanied the Roman soldiers to the Garden of Gethsemane.

We can therefore conclude that when the Roman soldiers and temple police arrived to arrest Jesus, the hillside where the Garden was located was literally covered with Roman soldiers and highly trained militia from the Temple Mount. I want you to really see what a huge crowd of armed men came that night, so let's look at what the other Gospels tell us about this same incident.

Matthew 26:47 says it was "a great multitude" of soldiers, using the Greek words *ochlos polus* to indicate that it was *a huge multitude* of armed men. Mark 14:43 calls it "a great multitude," using the Greek word *ochlos*, indicating that it was *a massive crowd*. Luke 22:47 also uses the word *ochlos*, indicating that the band of soldiers who came that night was *enormous*.

It makes one wonder what Judas had told the chief priests about Jesus that made them think they needed a small army to arrest Him! Did Judas forewarn them that Jesus and His disciples might put up a fight? Or is it possible that the chief priests were nervous that Jesus might use His supernatural power to resist them?

Certainly Jesus was known for His power. After all, He had ministered for three years, and miracles occurred wherever He went. The stories of Jesus' power must have already been legendary even during His lifetime here on earth.

Even Herod heard of Jesus' powers and longed to be an eyewitness of the miracles Jesus performed (*see* Luke 23:8). We saw what the apostle John said about this in John 21:25: The world itself couldn't contain all the books it would take to record every one of Jesus' miracles. So it's not too hard to imagine that the majority of people in Jesus' day had heard stories of the extraordinary power that flowed through Him.

It thrills my heart to think of the power of Jesus Christ! Even more thrilling is the knowledge that the same power that flowed through Him when He walked on this earth now flows through you and me. The same Holy Spirit who anointed Jesus to fulfill His ministry has been sent to empower us to do the same works He did! In fact, Jesus prophesied that we would do even *greater* works (John 14:12). This is the kind of power that operates in you and me!

Anytime the devil tries to insinuate that you're not a serious threat to be feared, you need to rise up and remind him that the Holy Spirit is your Power Source! Tell the devil (and remind yourself at the same time) that the Greater One lives inside you (1 John 4:4) and that you are a world overcomer (1 John 5:4).

Anytime the devil tries to insinuate that you're not a serious threat to be feared, you need to rise up and remind him that the Holy Spirit is your Power Source!

Remind yourself every day that the same power that raised Jesus from the dead now resides within you and is at your disposal 24 hours a day. Then the next time you're faced with a situation that needs to be turned around with supernatural power, open your heart and let that power flow — because the anointing that rested on Jesus when He walked this earth now rests on *you*!

Think About It

The mighty power that flowed through Jesus dwells inside you continually. When thoughts of failure and feelings of depression assail your mind, recognize them as an attack of the devil trying to make you believe you are less than who you are. You are a threat to the devil and his works because of the divine power that is at your disposal. Think about what that power will do when released into a situation — and then expect it to flow through you!

Satan was terrified of Jesus, and he revealed his fear of the Messiah long before the Garden of Gethsemane. When Jesus was born on this earth, the enemy inspired Herod the Great to slaughter all the babies in Bethlehem and the surrounding region in an attempt to kill Him.

A spirit of fear will always prompt people to overreact. Think about your own life for a moment. Are you facing an absurdly disproportionate amount of opposition against you right now because of your stand for God? If so, consider why the enemy is so afraid of what God plans to do through you!

How many times has the devil sought to destroy your life, your family, your business, or your ministry — but each time, you and yours eluded the enemy's grasp? What God-ordained purpose have you been preserved to fulfill? What has God instructed you to do in diligent preparation for that purpose to come to pass?

chapter

6

*Misunderstandings
and Suspicions*

chapter

6

Misunderstandings and Suspicions

Have you ever had an experience with someone who had a wrong perception of you? When you heard what that person thought of you, were you shocked to hear it? Did you wonder, *How could anyone ever think something like that about me?*

The more well-known you become, the more that people hear all kinds of rumors about you — most of which are completely untrue. You know how rumors work. When one person hears a rumor, he passes it along to another person, who then repeats it to someone else — and so it goes from one person to the next, growing more and more ridiculous with each telling. Finally, an entire story is being told that has no truth in it whatsoever. Unfortunately, when people hear a rumor, they usually believe it! *This is one reason Christians need to be very careful not to participate in gossip.*

I don't know what stories were being repeated about Jesus, but they must have been pretty wild. After all, when the Roman soldiers and temple police came to arrest Him in the Garden of Gethsemane, they were armed to the fullest extent! They also brought enough lanterns and torches to light up the entire Mount of Olives. What had they heard that made them think they needed to be so heavily equipped in order to find Jesus and the three disciples He'd brought along to pray with Him that night?

Judas had obviously prepared them for the worst. He had seen Jesus perform innumerable miracles, so he knew very well about the massive power that operated through Him. Judas had also been present in the past when religious leaders tried unsuccessfully to catch Jesus as He seemed to vanish, supernaturally slipping through the crowd to safety (Luke 4:30; John 8:59). Each time Jesus' enemies thought they had Him, but then suddenly — poof! He was gone!

When the troops arrived that night, they must have been operating on the basis of these stories. John 18:3 tells us, "Judas then, having received a band of men and officers from the chief priests and Pharisees, cometh thither with lanterns and torches and weapons."

I want to draw your attention to the words "lanterns," "torches," and "weapons." When you see the impact of these words, you'll understand that the soldiers who had come to arrest Jesus were acting on presumptions about Him that were totally inaccurate!

In the first place, Passover occurred at the time of a full moon, so the night was already very well lit at this time of year. But Judas didn't want to take a risk that Jesus and His disciples wouldn't be found; therefore, Judas obviously instructed these armed forces to be equipped to search, hunt, and track them down with the aid of "lanterns" and "torches."

The word "lantern" comes from the Greek word *phanos*. This word refers to *a bright and shining light*. It portrays something like a lamp stand — a light that is intended to "light up" a room so you can see things better. A *phanos* was actually the equivalent of a first-century flashlight. Its light was so brilliant that it penetrated darkened areas and revealed things hidden in darkness.

In addition to these lamps, John 18:3 tells us that the soldiers also carried "torches." The word "torch" is from the Greek word *lampas*, a word that describes *a long-burning oil lamp*. The "lamps" mentioned above were brilliant but short-lived. These "torches," however, were oil-based, had a long wick, and could burn all night if necessary. The fact that these soldiers came with these torches strongly suggests that the soldiers and police were prepared to search all night. So when they came to the Garden of Gethsemane that night, they had enough bright shining lights (*phanos*) and long-burning oil lamps (*lampas*) to hunt for Jesus all night long.

Several hundred soldiers scoured the hillside, carrying brightly lighted lamps as they searched for Jesus. This was the scene that occurred that night. Were the soldiers apprehensive that Jesus and His disciples might hide from them?

A great number of caverns, holes, and caves were scattered all over the hill where the Garden of Gethsemane was located. The hillside was also a place of many graves with large tombstones, behind which a person could hide. Finally, the hill offered prime hiding spots in its many great olive trees with twisted branches. So why in the world would 300 to 600 soldiers, plus the temple police, need so many brilliantly lit lights to find Jesus — unless they thought He would try to hide or escape from them?

John 18:3 also tells us that the soldiers and temple police brought "weapons" with them. The Greek word for "weapons" is *hoplos*, the very word that depicts *the full weaponry of a Roman soldier* referred to in Ephesians 6:13-18. This means the soldiers came attired in full weaponry — belt, breastplate, greaves, spikes, shoes, oblong shield, a brass helmet, a sword, and a lance. These 300 to 600 soldiers were ready for a *huge* skirmish and confrontation!

But there's still more to this story! In addition to the weapons the Roman soldiers bore that night, the temple police also came ready to put up a fight. Mark 14:43 says, "And immediately, while he yet spake, cometh Judas, one of the twelve, and with him a great multitude with swords and staves, from the chief priests and the scribes and the elders."

I want you to notice those words "swords" and "staves." The word "sword" is the Greek word *machaira*. It refers to *the most deadly type of sword*, one that was more often than not used for stabbing someone at close range. *Does this mean the temple police were ready to stab and draw blood that night?*

The word "stave" is from the Greek word *zhulos*. The word *zhulos* describes *a thick, heavy stick made of wood*. You might say it was a heavy-duty, dangerous, hard-hitting club intended to beat someone. When you look at the combined list of weapons brought to the Garden of Gethsemane that night, you will readily understand that these Roman soldiers and temple police were prepared to be militarily engaged!

As noted earlier, the stories being repeated about Jesus must have been pretty wild! What makes this even wilder is the likely prospect that Judas Iscariot was the one who fanned the flames of these rumors! He was right alongside the soldiers with all their lanterns, torches, and weapons.

Is it possible that after Judas had walked with Jesus for three years, he himself had never really come to know the real Jesus? Did Judas have a false perception of how Jesus would respond in such an event? It makes one wonder what kind of relationship Judas had with Jesus to perceive Him so inaccurately. The next two chapters will sufficiently answer this question regarding the kind of relationship Judas *really* had with Jesus.

As you know, Jesus willfully went with the soldiers that night. He and His disciples did *not* hide or put up a fight. After being supernaturally empowered by the angel God sent to help Him, Jesus rose up and went out to greet Judas and the troops. However, I'm personally convinced that when Jesus saw Judas surrounded by hundreds upon hundreds of soldiers and temple officers with lanterns, torches, and weapons, it must have stunned Him! I think Jesus was surprised to learn just how erroneously Judas perceived Him.

The next time you hear that someone has a wrong perception about you, don't let it ruffle your feathers too much. Remember all the times you've had a wrong perception about someone else! You were just so sure that your opinion about that person was right, but then you discovered you were so wrong! If you've perceived others incorrectly at times, why should it surprise you when the same thing occasionally happens to you?

If you ever find yourself in this position, consider it an opportunity to show people who you really are. Notice that Jesus didn't say to those who came for Him in the Garden, "How dare you think so badly about Me!" Instead of arguing or trying to prove a point, He simply surrendered, went with the soldiers, and gave His life for the very men who arrested Him. The response Jesus made with His life was the greatest comeback He could have demonstrated to them!

Instead of arguing or trying to prove a point, Jesus simply surrendered, went with the soldiers, and gave His life for the very men who arrested Him.

So when people misunderstand you, follow Jesus' example. Back off and take some time to think and pray about the matter before you proceed. Don't let the devil get you all upset because you were misunderstood. This may be the greatest chance you'll ever have to show people the truth about who you really are as a result of God's grace on your life!

Think About It

When people wrongfully judge us, we often want to retaliate with our words. But the best response comes from the way we live.

What is your life saying about you? Think about a time when the quality of your character invalidated a negative perception someone held about you. Did that misunderstanding affect the way you presented yourself and, in turn, perceived others?

The devil continually seeks to interject thoughts into our minds that will cause us to misinterpret the actions of another in order to create walls of division. When he succeeds in this strategy, the enemy prevents us from receiving from one another.

Have you ever misunderstood another person and then discovered you were wrong? What caused your initial perception of that person? What eventually proved it to be wrong? How could you have prevented such a misunderstanding in the first place?

Every day you are faced with opportunities to demonstrate the truth of who you really are. What do your words, attitudes, and actions reveal about you?

chapter

7

Kiss of Deception

chapter

7

Kiss of Deception

Have you ever been stabbed in the back by someone you thought was a true friend? You had walked with him and spent much time with him; you had shared your thoughts and even your secrets with him, thinking that everything you said would be held in confidence between the two of you. Then you discovered that the commitment you felt for that person was not what he felt for you. Can you recall any hurtful moments in your life like this?

This is what happened to Jesus on the night Judas betrayed Him. It was no accidental betrayal, but one that was premeditated and meticulously implemented. Before Judas led the soldiers and temple police to the Garden of Gethsemane, he met with the religious leaders and negotiated a deal for Jesus' capture.

During these meetings, Judas disclosed information about where Jesus prayed and where He met with His disciples. Judas must have also told them about Jesus' phenomenal power, which explains why so many soldiers came with weapons to arrest Jesus that night. It was in those meetings with the religious leaders that Judas agreed to receive a payment of 30 pieces of silver for delivering Jesus into their hands (Matthew 26:15; 27:9).

Because many of the soldiers and temple police had never seen Jesus before, Judas devised a special signal that would alert them to know who Jesus was. Mark 14:44 calls this special signal a "token," from the Greek word *sussemon*, meaning *a signal previously agreed upon*. This makes it emphatically clear that the kiss Judas gave Jesus was nothing more than a signal devised to let the troops know they needed to move swiftly to make their arrest.

Judas must have been very confused. On the one hand, he warned the religious leaders about Jesus' supernatural power so strongly that the soldiers arrived on the scene with weapons of murder, prepared to put up a serious fight. But on the other hand, Judas told them that he thought he could deliver Jesus into their hands with a mere kiss!

These two conflicting pictures provide an excellent example of the kind of confusion created inside a person who walks in deception. Deception is a powerful force that twists and distorts one's ability to see things clearly. Deceived people misperceive, misunderstand, misrepresent, and misjudge — and later don't even understand why they did what they did.

The different mixed signals Judas was giving about Jesus make it evident that Judas was both deceived and confused. He told the soldiers and temple police, "…Whomsoever I shall kiss, that same is he; take him, and lead him away safely" (Mark 14:44). The word "kiss" is the Greek word *phileo*. This well-known Greek word is used to show *strong emotion, affection, and love*. Later it came to represent such strong affection that it was used only between people who had *a strong bond* or *a deeply felt obligation* to each other, such as husbands and wives or family members. Still later, it came to be used as a form of greeting between especially dear and cherished friends.

During the time that the Gospels were written, the word *phileo* would have depicted *friends who were bound by some kind of obligation or covenant and who cherished each other very deeply*. On the basis of this deep emotion, it also became the Greek word for *a kiss* as a man would give his wife, as parents and children might give to each other, or as a brother or sister might give to his or her siblings.

In Mark 14:44, this word depicts not just a kiss of friendship, but a symbol of *deep love, affection, obligation, covenant, and relationship*. Giving this kind of kiss was a powerful symbol to everyone who saw it. Strangers would never greet each other with a kiss, for it was a greeting reserved only for the most special relationships. This is why Paul later told the Early Church in Rome to "salute one another with an holy kiss…" (Romans 16:16). It was a symbol in that day of deep affection, commitment, and covenant.

Judas knew beforehand that he could give Jesus such a kiss. This lets us know that he and Jesus were not strangers but had a unique, friendly relationship. As the bookkeeper and treasurer of the ministry, Judas had assuredly met often with Jesus to discuss ministry finances and disbursement of funds. It seems that during their three-year working relationship, they became dear and cherished friends — so close that Judas had the privilege of giving Jesus *a kiss* of friendship, a privilege reserved only for the intimate few in a person's life.

On the very night of Jesus' betrayal, He served Communion to all His disciples, including Judas Iscariot. That Communion was a reaffirmation of His covenant to all 12 disciples. Jesus understood what it meant to be in covenant. He knew He would have to lay down His life to empower that covenant and make it real. And just as Jesus reaffirmed His covenant to the other disciples that night, He also confirmed it to Judas. Jesus extended His genuine love and commitment to Judas as He offered him the bread and wine, and Judas feigned commitment by accepting the bread and the wine as symbols of the covenant.

> *Jesus extended His genuine love and commitment to Judas as He offered him the bread and wine, and Judas feigned commitment by accepting the bread and the wine as symbols of the covenant.*

However, Judas' loyalty to Jesus was fatally flawed. As noted above, that night Judas told the troops and temple police, "…Whomsoever I shall kiss, that same is he; take him, and lead him away safely" (Mark 14:44).

Betraying Jesus with a kiss was about as low as a person could go. It was like saying, "You and I are friends forever. Now please turn around so I can sink my dagger into your back!" You see, the kiss Judas gave was a false kiss that revealed insincerity, bogus love, and a phony commitment. The fact that it was premeditated made it even worse. This was no last-minute, accidental betrayal; it was well-planned and very deliberate. Judas played the game all the way to the end, working closely with Jesus and remaining a part of His inner circle. Then at the preappointed time, Judas drove in the dagger as deeply as he could.

When I travel and speak with people, I repeatedly hear stories of those who have felt betrayed by someone they dearly loved and trusted. Although they never gave the other person a kiss as a symbol of their affection, they opened their hearts, shared their secrets, and gave a part of themselves to him or her. Then later they discovered that the person they loved and trusted wasn't as he or she seemed. That kind of discovery can be a very traumatic and emotional ordeal.

Have you ever experienced betrayal somewhere along the way from a friend or an associate you thought was a true friend — only to find out later that he or she wasn't? Did you wonder, *How could this person behave like this after we've been together for so long?*

Something was evidently wrong in the relationship from the beginning. Maybe you subconsciously knew something was wrong, but you loved the person so much that you didn't want to see what your heart was telling you. Or perhaps you really were blind to what was happening right under your nose.

When someone betrays you, you can be certain that: 1) the person was never who you thought he or she was to begin with, or 2) you sensed something wasn't right but allowed yourself to go ahead with the relationship anyway.

Does either of these scenarios describe something you've experienced? Have you been burned by someone you trusted? If you allow your hurt to fester and grow inside you, it will only make you bitter and ugly. It's time for you to forgive and let go of that offense so you can move on with your life.

Jesus always knew that Judas would be His betrayer; nevertheless, Jesus loved Judas, working closely with him and even sharing Communion with him on the same night of Judas' betrayal!

You may ask, *Why did Jesus extend so much of Himself to someone He knew would be disloyal to Him?* Let me answer this question by posing a few questions to you:

- ❖ Have you ever been disloyal and unfaithful to Jesus?

- ❖ Have you ever violated His authority in your life by disobeying Him?

- ❖ Have you ever dragged Him into unholy situations that you'd gotten yourself into?

- ❖ Have you ever betrayed or denied Him in your own life?

If you're honest, your answer to all four of these questions will be "Yes, I've done that!" Jesus knew you would do these things even before He called you and saved you. But did He throw you out, reject you, or disown you? No, He forgave you, and He is still forgiving you now. Aren't you glad that Jesus has so much patience with you? Aren't you grateful He gives you so many chances to get things right?

So just learn from the experience, and determine to never let a Judas be your best friend again. Then allow the Holy Spirit to lead you to the finest friends you've ever had in your life!

Yes, it is certainly painful to feel betrayed by someone close to you. But if you'll allow this experience to work for you and not against you, it will make you a stronger and better person. And when you come out on the other side, you'll be in a position to understand what others are going through who have been hurt by betrayal so you can be a help and a blessing to them.

Think About It

Accidental betrayal is one thing, but premeditated disloyalty is another. What steps can you take to ensure your heart remains loyal to Jesus?

Jesus knew that Judas would betray Him; nevertheless, Jesus continued to work closely with Judas.

Can you recall a time when you sensed someone was not authentic, yet you chose to continue a relationship with him or her anyway? In retrospect, was that decision directed by the Spirit of God, or was it the result of not heeding the Holy Spirit's direction?

The act of betrayal reveals the quality of a person's character, whether he is the betrayer or the one betrayed. Have you ever betrayed someone or been betrayed by another? If so, what did you learn about yourself as a result of that experience? How has it changed you?

chapter

8

*Test of Loyalty,
Test of Love*

8

Test of Loyalty, Test of Love

When I was a young man and just getting started in the ministry, God positioned me under a great man of God who could read Greek and exegete New Testament verses and was strongly anointed by the Spirit of God. To me, this minister had the best combination possible — brains and anointing all mixed together in one package! The first time I heard him preach, my jaw dropped open! His preaching reminded me of the way Jesus baffled the scribes when they heard Him teach with such great authority. I immediately knew that I needed to be under this man's anointing and to receive from his life.

God opened the door for me to be trained by this great man of God, and for two years I worked side by side with him every day — carrying his books and traveling to his meetings with him. I literally met with him seven days a week so he could teach and train me. It was amazing that a man of this caliber would put so much of himself into someone as young as I was, but he did it because he believed in the call of God on my life. This man imparted the tools, the skills, and the understanding I needed to become a man of God who could both grow in the things of the Spirit and establish a ministry that was balanced between the Word and the Spirit.

Everything was great between this minister and me — until one day when I got offended. The reason for the offense is not important, but the situation revealed that I had a flaw in my understanding of authority and submission.

This was an expensive lesson that God has used throughout the years of my ministry as I have worked with others who are themselves learning the hard lessons of submission and authority. Because of what I experienced, I understand the temptation people occasionally feel to think too highly of themselves and to run off and leave their spiritual mentors.

That is exactly what I did to this man who had been so gracious to me. After he had poured his life into me, teaching and training me, I left him when we had our first major disagreement. Although I called him my pastor, the conflict between us revealed that I had never really given him a place of authority in my life. He had been a great example to me, and I respected him as the best teacher I had ever heard. Yet I had obviously never received him as God's authority in my life; if I had, I never would have done what I did to him.

Unfortunately, the true level of one's commitment isn't tested by good times, but by times of conflict and disagreement. It's easy to walk together when you agree with the one you call your spiritual authority and you're having a good time together. But what happens when you disagree or experience a conflict in your relationship? This is the critical moment when the truth about your level of submission will become observable.

When Judas Iscariot came to the Garden of Gethsemane the night he betrayed Jesus, he said something that revealed he had never been truly submitted to Him. The truth about Judas' recognition of and submission to Jesus' authority was exposed that night, just as my submission to that minister was also proven to be defective. Mark 14:45 says, "And as soon as he [Judas] was come, he goeth straightway to him, and saith, Master, master; and kissed him."

Notice that Judas called Jesus, "Master, master." These words reveal the type of relationship that *really* existed in Judas' heart toward Jesus.

These words also reveal the reason the devil was able to use Judas, and not one of the other disciples, to betray Jesus.

The word "master" comes from the Greek word *didaskalos*, which means *teacher*. When it is translated "master," as in this verse, it is intended to give the idea of *one who is a fabulous, masterful teacher*. This is the Greek equivalent of the Hebrew word *rabbi*. Of course, a *rabbi* is a teacher who is honored and respected because of his understanding of and ability to explain the Scriptures. When Judas approached Jesus in the Garden that night, this is exactly the title he used when he referred to Jesus. He called Him, "Master, master." It literally meant, "Teacher, teacher."

Titles are very important because they define relationships. For instance, the words "Daddy" and "Mother" define the unique relationship between a child and a parent. The word "Boss" defines the relationship between an employee and his employer — a relationship much different than the one that exists between the employee and his fellow employees. The words "Mr. President" define the relationship between the nation and its leader. The word "Pastor" defines the relationship between a congregation and their pastor.

A world without titles would be a world with confusion, for titles give rank, order, and definition to relationships. Jesus Himself told the disciples, "Ye call me Master and Lord: and ye say well; for so I am" (John 13:13). Even Jesus acknowledged it was correct for His disciples to call Him "Lord" and "Master." In fact, there isn't a single occurrence in the Gospels where they called Him "Jesus." They were always respectful, honoring, and deferential when they spoke of Him or to Him.

But I want you to notice what title Judas *didn't* use that night — he didn't call Jesus "Lord." The word for "lord" expresses the idea of *one who has ultimate and supreme authority in your life*. If you called someone "lord," it would mean you were submitted to that person's authority and had yielded every realm of your life to his management, direction, and control.

Had Judas called Jesus "Lord" that night, it would have meant that Judas had surrendered his life to Jesus' control and was submitted to His authority. But Judas *didn't* use the word "Lord." He used the word for "Teacher," which revealed that Jesus had never really become God's authority in Judas' life. The truth is, Judas had only received Jesus as a Teacher, a Rabbi, and a gifted Communicator, but never as Lord.

As happens in all relationships where submission to authority is required, the moment finally came that proved the true level of Judas' submission to Jesus. When the test came, Judas failed it. There was a fatal flaw in his relationship with Jesus. In the end, it became apparent to everyone that even though Judas honored and followed Jesus as a Master Teacher, Jesus had never been his Lord. Thus, Judas' side of his relationship with Jesus had been artificial from the very beginning.

Jesus knew what was in the heart of Judas, yet continued to work closely with him, extending unfathomable mercy, amazing grace, and astounding patience toward him. Jesus graciously extended His time and attention to Judas to correct the fatal flaws in the disciple's character and to help him get things right.

Even with all of Jesus' love and patience, the ball was in Judas' court. The disciple was the one who ultimately determined the level of relationship that would exist between himself and Jesus.

But even with all of Jesus' love and patience, the ball was in Judas' court. The disciple was the one who ultimately determined the level of relationship that would exist between himself and Jesus. Jesus was willing to be Judas' Lord — but Judas was never truly willing to be in submission to Jesus' authority. Instead, Judas only authorized Jesus to be a gifted Teacher in his life.

I have learned over the years that it takes time to really get to know who people are. The apostle Paul urged us not to lay hands on people suddenly for this very reason (1 Timothy 5:22).

So don't be too shocked if you discover that someone you thought was with you all the way really isn't with you at all. *If this ever happens to you, remember that it happened to Jesus too.* Just as God used Jesus to extend mercy, grace, and patience to Judas Iscariot, God may be using you now to give an unfaithful person a chance to have a change of heart so he can become *faithful*.

Can God count on you to be His extension of kindness to that person? Are you to be His mercy outstretched to give that person a magnificent opportunity to make a true turnaround in his heart, mind, and character?

When I wronged my pastor so many years ago, my actions uncovered a flaw inside me that needed correction. It revealed that I didn't understand what submission to authority really meant. In retrospect, I'm so thankful that this happened, for God used it to expose a defect in my character that needed to be eradicated. To change me, He tapped a great man of God on the shoulder and instructed him to love me, forgive me, and teach me. Because he was willing to be God's outstretched hand of mercy in my life, I *was* corrected, delivered, and changed. I can never thank God enough for placing me under a person who cared enough for me to stick with me and bring correction into my life.

Are *you* supposed to be that kind of person to someone close to you right now? It's so easy to fixate on the kiss of betrayal, but just think about how much God loves that "problem person" in your life. He is trying to help him by giving him a friend like you!

If that person chooses *not* to respond to the mercy, grace, and patience that are being poured out to him through you, he will have to live with the results of his decision. Just make sure that you fulfill what God is requiring of *you* in this relationship. It may seem difficult to do, but you need to be thankful that God has kindly entrusted you with the responsibility of giving a person who has been unfaithful another chance.

Think About It

People who do not effectively understand submission and authority can be difficult to deal with in business, in marriage, in ministry, and in life. If such a person is in your life, how are you responding to help that individual grow and change for the better? What have you discovered about your own heart in the process?

Titles give rank, order, and definition to relationships. What title does Jesus really hold in your personal life? The answer is found in the ways and in the areas you submit to Him. Are there areas of your life where you reserve the right to have the last word?

Think about the mentors and influences God has brought into your life through the years to teach and train you so you can fulfill your divine purpose. What are some significant ways you can express honor to these mentors for their role in your life? Have you allowed an offense to separate you from any of these individuals? If so, what steps can you take to mend that breach?

chapter

9

Paralyzed by His Presence

chapter

9

Paralyzed by His Presence

Just as the Roman soldiers and temple police were preparing to arrest Jesus, a supernatural power was suddenly released that was so strong, it literally threw an entire band of 300 to 600 soldiers backward and down onto the ground! It was as if an invisible bomb had been detonated. So much explosive strength was released that the force of that power knocked the soldiers flat on their backs! Where did this discharge of power come from, and what released it?

After Jesus received Judas' kiss of betrayal, He stepped forward and asked the crowd of militia, "...Whom seek ye? They answered him, Jesus of Nazareth. Jesus saith unto them, I am he.... As soon then as he had said unto them, I am he, *they went backward, and fell to the ground*" (John 18:4-6).

Notice how Jesus identified himself. He told them, *"I am he."* These mighty words come from the Greek words *ego eimi*, which is more accurately translated, "I AM!" It was not the first time Jesus used this phrase to identify Himself; He also used it in John 8:58 and John 13:19. When the hearers of that day heard those words *ego eimi*, they immediately recognized them as the very words God used to identify Himself when He spoke to Moses on Mount Horeb in Exodus 3:14.

But let's look at the two additional examples of the word *ego eimi* in the Gospel of John. In John 8:58, Jesus said, "Verily, verily, I say unto you, Before Abraham was, I am." Those final words in the verse, "I am," are the Greek words *ego eimi* and should be translated, "I AM!"

In John 13:19, Jesus said, "Now I tell you before it come, that, when it is come to pass, ye may believe that I am he." If you read the *King James Version*, you will notice that the word "he" is italicized, meaning it was supplied by the *King James* translators and is not in the original. The Greek simply says, "...Ye may believe that I AM!" In both of these cited texts, Jesus strongly and boldly affirmed that He was the Great "I AM" of the Old Testament.

Now in John 18:5 and 6, Jesus uses the words *ego eimi* again. The soldiers wanted to know, *"Who are you?"* They probably expected him to answer, "Jesus of Nazareth" — but instead, He answered, "I AM!" John 18:6 tells us, "As soon then as he had said unto them, I am he, they went backward, and fell to the ground." A more accurate rendering would be *"As soon then as he said unto them, I AM, they went backward and fell to the ground."*

The words "went backward" come from the Greek word *aperchomai.* In this case, the words depict the soldiers and temple police *staggering* and *stumbling backward*, as if some force had hit them and was pushing them backward. The word "fell" is the Greek word *pipto*, which means *to fall*. It was often used to depict *a person who fell so hard, it appeared that he fell dead or fell like a corpse.*

The members of this militia that came to arrest Jesus were knocked flat by some kind of invisible force. In fact, the verse says they went backward and fell "to the ground." The words "to the ground" are taken from the Greek word *chamai*, which depicts these soldiers falling abruptly and hitting the ground *hard*. Some force unexpectedly, suddenly, and forcefully knocked these troops and temple police flat!

Think of it — 300 to 600 Roman soldiers and a large number of trained temple police had all come laden with weapons, swords, and clubs to help them capture Jesus. After they announced that they were searching for Jesus of Nazareth, Jesus answered them with the words, "I AM," thus identifying Himself as the "I AM" of the Old Testament. And when Jesus spoke those words, a great blast of God's power was unleashed —

so strong that it literally thrust the troops and police backward, causing them to stagger, wobble, and stumble as they hit the ground hard.

What a shock it must have been for those military men! They discovered that the mere words of Jesus were enough to overwhelm and overpower them! The tales they had heard about Jesus' power were correct. Of course He really was strong enough to overcome an army. After all, He was the Great "I AM"!

After Jesus proved He couldn't be taken by force, He willfully surrendered to them, knowing it was all a part of the Father's plan for the redemption of mankind. But it's important to understand that *no one took Jesus*. It was His *voluntary choice* to go with the troops.

The Jesus we serve is powerful! There is no force strong enough to resist His power. No sickness, financial turmoil, relational problems, political force — *absolutely nothing* has enough power to resist the supernatural power of Jesus Christ! When the Great "I AM" opens His mouth and speaks, every power that attempts to defy Him or His Word is pushed backward and shaken until it staggers, stumbles, and falls to the ground! Yet although the soldiers couldn't take Jesus by force, He willingly went with them for you and me.

When the Great "I AM" opens His mouth and speaks, every power that attempts to defy Him or His Word is pushed backward and shaken until it staggers, stumbles, and falls to the ground!

What is your need today? Why not present those needs to Jesus, the Great "I AM"? Let Him speak to your heart, directing you to His Word. Once you see the promise you need for the specific situation you're facing, get your mouth in agreement with His Word. As you do, you, too, will see the mighty power of God unleashed against the evil forces that try to defy you!

Think About It

Life and death are in the power of the tongue (Proverbs 18:21). Are you faced with a situation — sickness, lack, confusion, or sin — that is defying the will of God in your life? See that problem as a mountain before you, and then speak God's Word to unleash the mighty force of His power against the forces of the enemy trying to oppose you.

Jesus boldly affirmed who He was, and His attackers fell backward. When you boldly affirm who you are in Christ, attacks against your life will fall backward as well. Consider some ways in which you can be bolder in your affirmation of who God is — and who He is in you.

Consider the supernatural power that is released when you speak Jesus' name. How can you actively release that power into your life, as well as into the lives of others? Are you being faithful to do that?

chapter

10

The Danger of Taking Matters Into Your Own Hands

chapter

10

The Danger
of Taking Matters
Into Your Own Hands

Can you think of a time when you became so impatient while waiting on the Lord that you decided to take matters into your own hands to get things moving a little faster? When you later realized that you had made a big mess of things, were you regretful that you didn't wait a little longer before taking action?

At one time or another, all of us have been guilty of acting rashly and thoughtlessly. For example, just think of how many times you've said something you later regretted. Oh, how you wished you could retract those words, but it was too late! Or perhaps you've been guilty of acting spontaneously on an issue before you had enough time to really think things through.

Or have you ever gotten so angry at someone that you popped off and vocalized your dissent before the other person was finished talking? When you later realized that the person wasn't saying what you thought, did you feel like a fool for reacting too quickly? Did you have to apologize for making a rash statement, all the while wishing you had just kept your mouth shut a few minutes longer?

Hotheaded moments rarely produce good fruit. In fact, when we act rashly, we usually end up loathing the stupidity of our words and actions. The truth is, we all need a good dose of patience — a fruit that is produced inside us by the Spirit of God. We desperately need patience in our lives!

Perhaps no story better demonstrates the mess that impatience produces than that night in the Garden of Gethsemane when Peter seized a sword, swung it with all his might, and lopped off the ear of the high priest's servant.

When Jesus spoke and identified Himself as the great "I AM," the soldiers and temple police were knocked to the ground — their eyes dazed, their heads whirling and spinning, and their bodies stunned by the power of God. The power that was released hit them so hard and so fast that they were on their backs before they knew what happened!

While these soldiers were still flat on their backs, Peter suddenly decided to take matters into his own hands. He must have seen it as his great chance to show himself brave and to take advantage of the moment, but what he did was simply shocking! It is the perfect picture of someone acting before thinking things all the way through.

Peter's spontaneous, hasty behavior earned him a place in history that no one has ever forgotten. However, to see the full picture of what happened that night, it is essential to piece the story together from both Luke's and John's Gospel, for each Gospel writer tells a different part of the story.

While the soldiers and temple police were lying on their backs, Peter looked around and realized that the armed men were disabled. So he pulled out his own sword, and with sword in hand, gleefully asked, "...Lord, shall we smite with the sword?" (Luke 22:49).

Before Jesus had an opportunity to answer, Peter swung into action and did something outrageous and utterly bizarre! He gripped the sword and impulsively swung down, slicing right past the head of the high priest's servant. Imagine how shocked Jesus must have been to see Peter lop off this poor man's ear and then to watch the severed ear fall into the dirt on the ground! John 18:10 tells us that Peter "...smote the high priest's servant, and cut off his right ear...."

Let's look at these words to see exactly what happened in that impulsive moment when Peter swung this sword. The word "smote" is the Greek word *epaio*, from the word *paio*, and it means *to strike*, as a person who viciously strikes someone with a dangerous tool, weapon, or instrument. It can also be translated *to sting*, like a scorpion that strongly injects its stinger into a victim. In addition, it means *to beat with the fist*. In this verse, the word is used to picture *the force* of Peter's swinging action. This tells us that Peter put all his strength into the swinging of his sword, fully intending to cause some kind of bodily impairment.

Do you think Peter was aiming for the servant's ear? Why would anyone attack an ear? Furthermore, it wouldn't take this much force to cut off an ear. No, I believe Peter was aiming for the man's head and missed, swiping the man's ear by mistake. When that sword missed its target, it slipped down the side of the servant's head and took his ear with it.

When John 18:10 says Peter "cut off" his right ear, the words "cut off" are from the Greek word *apokopto*, which is a compound of the words *apo* and *kopto*. The word *apo* means *away*, and the word *kopto* means *to cut downward*. Put together, the new word describes *a downward swing that cuts something off*. In this case, Peter swung downward so hard that he completely removed the ear of the servant of the high priest.

Some try to insinuate that Peter merely nipped this man's ear, but the Greek shows that the swing of Peter's sword caused the ear's complete removal. The Greek word for "ear" is *otarion*, and it refers to *the entire outer ear*. The Bible is so detailed about the events that occurred that night, it even tells us it was the servant's *right* ear. The servant of the high priest lost his entire right ear when Peter swung in his direction!

John 18:10 tells us the servant's name was *Malchus*. Who was this Malchus? Did Peter indiscriminately select Malchus as his target that night? Was there a particular reason Peter chose this man as the focus of his wrath?

The name Malchus has two meanings: *ruler* and *counselor*. We don't know that this was the servant's original name. It may have been a name given to him because of his close position to the high priest, who at that time was a man named Caiaphas. Caiaphas was a member of the Sadducees, a sect that was particularly opposed to the reality of supernatural happenings, viewing most supernatural events of the Old Testament as myths and legends. This is one reason Caiaphas was so antagonistic to the ministry of Jesus, which, of course, was overflowing with miraculous events every day.

When Peter saw Malchus in the Garden of Gethsemane, it no doubt brought back memories of the many times he had seen Malchus standing at the side of the high priest. Although this man is referred to as the servant of the high priest, he in fact was the high priest's personal assistant. This was a very prominent position in the religious order of the priesthood. As a high-ranking officer of the religious court, Malchus was regally dressed and carried himself with pride and dignity. To Peter's eye, he probably represented everything that belonged to the realm of the priesthood, an order of religious men that had instigated numerous problems for Jesus and His disciples.

Because Malchus was present at the time of Jesus' arrest, we may conclude that he was sent as the personal representative of the high priest to officially oversee the activities connected with Jesus' arrest. Few scholars believe that Peter singled him out by chance. Although the following thought can't be said with absolute certainty, Malchus may have become the intended target because of Peter's deep resentment and long-held grudge toward the high priest and his entourage, all of whom had been continually critical of Jesus' ministry.

I must point out that the healing of Malchus' ear was the last miracle Jesus performed during His earthly ministry. What a statement this makes to us about Jesus! Just before He went to the Cross, He reached out to help a publicly declared and avowed foe!

This man was part of a group that had been menacing and antagonistic toward Jesus. But Jesus didn't say, *"Finally, one of you guys got what you deserve!"* Instead, He reached out to the man in his need, touched him, and *supernaturally* healed him. Keep in mind that the high priest, a Sadducee, was vehemently opposed to Jesus' supernatural ministry. Yet it was the high priest's own servant who received *a supernatural touch* from Jesus!

> *More than likely, Peter acted out of a long-held offense, but Jesus demonstrated love and genuine care even to those who opposed Him during His life and who were instrumental in leading Him to His crucifixion.*

What a contrast Jesus' actions were to Peter's behavior! More than likely, Peter acted out of a long-held offense, but Jesus demonstrated love and genuine care even to those who opposed Him during His life and who were instrumental in leading Him to His crucifixion.

So don't follow Peter's example in the Garden of Gethsamene. Instead, pray for the grace to be like Jesus! Decide today to let the Holy Spirit empower you to reach out in forgiveness to those who have offended you or caused you harm. Determine to love your offenders and opponents the way Jesus loves them.

Think About It

It is the goodness of God that draws people to repentance (Romans 2:4). Is there a person or a group of people who are antagonistic toward you? How have they made their negative intent toward you known? In what ways are you allowing the Holy Spirit to equip you to reach out to them in love?

In a moment of rashness, Peter cut off a man's ear. Can you think of times when you acted out of haste without thinking through the root and the results of your actions? Thinking back on those times and the consequences that followed, can you think of alternate ways that you should have responded to those situations?

When we refuse to wait on God, impatience will always produce a problem in our lives. By taking matters into our own hands, we often dig a hole so deep for ourselves that only He can get us out.

Every choice has a consequence. Are you making the choices today that will produce the results you want tomorrow?

chapter

11

Jesus Cleans Up Peter's Mess!

11

Jesus Cleans Up Peter's Mess!

Have you ever had a time when it nearly broke your heart to see what a mess a friend had made of his life? Because you loved your friend so much, you were willing to do anything necessary to assist him in getting his life back in order again. Although you knew it would be difficult, you were nonetheless willing to step into his disorder, chaos, and confusion to help him because you knew he'd never get out of his mess by himself.

Let's see what Jesus did for Peter that night in the Garden of Gethsemane after Peter chopped off the ear of Malchus, the servant of the high priest. There is something we can learn from the example Jesus gave us that night.

What Peter did to Malchus was not only scandalous — it was against the law and therefore punishable. Peter's action was criminal! Peter's wrongdoing was sufficient to ruin his entire life, since he could have been sentenced for physically injuring a fellow citizen. And this wasn't just any citizen. As the servant of the high priest, Malchus was an extremely well-known man in the city of Jerusalem. Peter certainly would have been imprisoned for injuring a person of such stature.

Jesus had just been sweating blood from the intense spiritual battle He fought in prayer in the Garden. Then He had received the kiss of betrayal from a friend and was therefore facing the prospect of the Cross and three days in the grave. Now a new problem had been thrust upon Him. Because of Peter's impetuous, unauthorized behavior, Jesus had to put everything on hold for a moment so He could step forward and fix the mess Peter had created!

Because of Peter's impetuous, unauthorized behavior, Jesus had to put everything on hold for a moment so He could step forward and fix the mess Peter had created!

As blood poured from the side of Malchus' head and dripped from the blade Peter held in his hand, Jesus asked the soldiers, "...Suffer ye thus far..." (Luke 22:51). This was the equivalent of saying, *"Let Me just do one more thing before you take Me!"*

Then Jesus reached out to Malchus and "...touched his ear, and healed him." Rather than allow Himself to be taken away while Peter was still subject to arrest, imprisonment, and possible execution, Jesus stopped the entire process to fix the mess Peter made that night.

The Bible says that Jesus "touched" the servant. The Greek word for "touch" is *aptomai*, a word that means *to firmly grasp* or *to hold tightly*. This is very important, for it lets us know that Jesus didn't just lightly touch Malchus; He firmly grabbed the servant's head and held it tightly.

Why is this so significant? Because it tells us the tenacity with which Jesus prayed. When He laid His hands on people, they *knew* that hands had been laid on them!

The Bible doesn't tell us whether Jesus touched the stump that remained from the severed ear and grew a new ear or grabbed the old ear from the ground and miraculously set it back in its place. Regardless of how the miracle occurred, however, the word *aptomai* ("touched") lets us know that Jesus was aggressive in the way He touched the man.

As a result of Jesus' touch, Malchus was completely "healed" (v. 51). The word "healed" is the Greek word *iaomai*, which means *to cure, to restore*, or *to heal*. Jesus completely restored Malchus' ear before the soldiers bound Him and led Him out of the Garden.

That night in the Garden of Gethsemane, Jesus' very words knocked 300 to 600 soldiers off their feet and flat on their backs. He didn't need Peter's help. He didn't request Peter's intervention. Nevertheless, Peter suddenly jumped in the middle of God's business and tried to instigate a revolt. Yet rather than walk off and leave Peter in the mess he had made by his own doings, Jesus stopped everything that was happening and intervened on His disciple's behalf. Jesus took the time to heal Malchus' ear for two primary reasons: 1) because He *is* a Healer, and 2) because He didn't want Peter to be arrested for his impulsive actions.

The next time you think you are too busy or too important to get involved in a friend's problem, remember this example that Jesus gave us on the night of His arrest. That night Jesus had a lot on His mind, but He still stopped everything to help a friend. He could have said, *"Peter, you've made this mess by yourself; now you can fix it by yourself."* But it was clear that Peter would never get out of this trouble without assistance, so Jesus stepped in to help Peter get things back in order again.

When you are tempted to be judgmental about other people's self-imposed problems, it would be good for you to remember the many times God's mercy has intervened to save you from messy situations that you created yourself. Even though you deserved to get in trouble, God loved you enough to come right alongside you and help you pull things together so you could get out of that mess. Now whenever you see others in trouble, you have the opportunity to be an extension of God's mercy to them.

Put everything on hold for a few minutes so you can reach out to a friend in trouble; then do whatever you can to help restore the situation. If this was important enough for Jesus to do, then you have time to do it as well. Make it a priority today to be a faithful friend to the end, just as Jesus was to Peter in the Garden of Gethsemane!

Think About It

The only thing more frustrating and painful than making a mistake or going through a difficult time is watching someone you care about go through difficulty — particularly when it's a situation of his or her own design. There are times when people need someone to step in and help them get their lives in order again.

Can you think of a time when you were in trouble and someone helped you fix your situation without smothering you in judgment for what may have been a self-imposed problem? How did that person's intervention affect you then, and how does his or her example of love continue to influence you today?

Usually when a person needs your help the most, it isn't convenient for you to step in. Jesus was in the midst of an intense spiritual battle in the Garden of Gethsemane, and Peter's actions only further complicated the situation. Notice that Jesus put His own pain on pause to correct the chaos as He brought healing to Malchus and help to Peter.

How do you respond to others around you when, in the midst of trying to deal with your own personal dilemma, you see someone making a mess in his or her life or observe someone suffering? Does your response mirror the way that Jesus responded to Peter?

Jesus is a faithful Friend. Every day His mercy is available to intervene in your life — pulling you out of problems, pulling your life together. Are you honoring the sacrifice Jesus made for you by receiving His merciful intervention in your life? Take some time to think about that, and then consider how you can be an extension of God's mercy to someone else today.

chapter
12
Twelve Legions of Angels

chapter

12

Twelve Legions of Angels

$\mathcal{How}$ much strength do you think one angel possesses?

To answer that question, I want you to consider the full impact of Jesus' words in Matthew 26:53, where He said, "Thinkest thou that I cannot now pray to my Father, and he shall presently give me more than twelve legions of angels?"

To fully understand the magnitude of what Jesus said here, we need to know:

1. What is a "legion"?

2. How many angels would there be in 12 legions?

3. What would be the combined strength of this number of angels?

It is important to answer these questions, because the answers reveal the full might that was available to Jesus had He requested supernatural help in the Garden of Gethsemane. Actually, when we take into account the power that was already demonstrated in the Garden and then add the potential assistance and impact of 12 legions of angels, it becomes obvious that there was no human force on earth strong enough to take Jesus against His will. The only way He was going to be taken was if He *allowed* Himself to be taken! This is why Jesus later told Pilate, "...Thou couldest have no power at all against me, except it were given thee from above..." (John 19:11).

Let's begin with our first question: *What is a "legion"?* The word "legion" is a military term that was taken from the Roman army. A legion denoted a group of at least 6,000 Roman soldiers, although the total number could be higher. This means that anytime we read about a legion of anything, we can know it always refers to at least 6,000 of something.

An amazing example of this is found in Mark 5:9, where the Bible tells us that the demon-possessed man of the Gadarenes had a legion of demons. That means this man had an infestation of at least 6,000 demons residing inside him!

Let's now contemplate the second question: *How many angels would there be in 12 legions?* Since the word "legion" refers to *at least* 6,000, it means a legion of angels would be *at least* 6,000 angels. However, Jesus said the Father would give Him "more than" 12 legions of angels if He requested it. Because it would be pure speculation to try to figure out how many "more than" 12 legions would be, let's just stick with the figure of 12 legions to see how many angels that entails.

One legion is 6,000 angels, so if you simply multiply that number by 12, you'll discover that 12 legions of angels would include a minimum of *72,000 angels*. But Jesus said the Father would give Him *more than* 12 legions of angels. Therefore, you can conclude that there were potentially many additional thousands of angels available to Jesus the night He was arrested!

Finally, let's look at our third question: *What would be the combined strength in this number of angels?* Angels are powerful! In fact, Isaiah 37:36 records that a single angel obliterated 185,000 men in one night. So if a single angel had that kind of power, how much combined strength would there be in 12 legions of angels?

Since a single angel was able to obliterate 185,000 men in one night, that means the combined strength in a legion of 6,000 angels would be enough to destroy 1,110,000,000 men (that is, 1 billion, 110 million men) — and that's just the combined power in *one* legion of angels!

Now let's multiply this same number 185,000 by 12 legions, or at least 72,000 angels, which was the number of angels Jesus said was available to Him on the night of His arrest. When we do, we find that there was enough combined strength at Jesus' disposal to have annihilated at least 13,320,000,000 men (that is, 13 billion, 320 million men) — which is more than twice the number of people living on the earth right now!

Of course, this is assuming that the angel spoken of in Isaiah 37:36 had maxed out his power at 185,000 men (which is unlikely). Simply put, angels are *powerful*, and Jesus had a *huge* number of angels at His disposal!

Jesus didn't need Peter's little sword that night. Had He chosen to do so, Jesus could have summoned 72,000 magnificent, mighty, dazzling, glorious, overwhelmingly powerful angels to the Garden to obliterate the Roman soldiers and the temple police who had come to arrest Him. In fact, the combined strength in 12 legions of angels could have wiped out the entire human race! But Jesus *didn't* call on the supernatural help that was available to Him. Why? Because He knew it was time for Him to voluntarily lay down His life for the sin of the human race.

> *Jesus didn't call on the supernatural help that was available to Him. Why? Because He knew it was time for Him to voluntarily lay down His life for the sin of the human race.*

Learn a lesson from Jesus and from the apostle Peter. Jesus didn't need Peter's undersized, insignificant sword to deal with His situation. What good would a single sword have been against all the troops assembled in the Garden that night anyway? Peter's actions were a perfect example of how the flesh tries in vain to solve its own problems but cannot. Jesus had all the power that was needed to conquer those troops.

As you face your own challenges in life, always keep in mind that Jesus has the power to fix any problem you'll ever come across. Before you jump in and make things worse by taking matters into your own hands, remember the story of Peter! The next time you're tempted to "grab a sword and start swinging," take a few minutes to remind yourself that Jesus can handle the problem without your intervention. Before you do anything else, *pray* and ask the Lord what you are supposed to do. Then after you receive your answer and follow His instructions, just watch His supernatural power swing into action to solve the dilemma you are facing!

Think About It

When we think of the potential power available to Jesus through angelic assistance alone, it seems almost laughable that Peter thought his little sword offered protection. Yet all of us have made similar mistakes at times in our own lives.

The same Holy Spirit who raised Jesus from the dead is within you, and the same power available to Him is also available to you. What pitifully inadequate substitutes for God's power have you attempted to rely on in the past when you faced a difficult situation and were in need of divine help and deliverance?

Man's natural tendency is always to try to solve his own problems. Consider your own patterns and history of natural attempts to solve situations. In what ways could you have looked to the Lord and allowed His power to resolve what you could not?

If you are a believer, you already have all the power at your disposal to fix any problem you'll ever come across. Consider the greatest challenge you're facing at this moment. Pray and ask God for His supernatural assistance. Then "put away your sword" and follow His instructions.

chapter

13

Who Was the Naked Boy in the Garden of Gethsemane?

chapter

13

Who Was the Naked Boy in the Garden of Gethsemane?

Just about the time Jesus finished healing the ear of the servant of the high priest named Malchus, the Gospel of Mark tells us a naked young man was found in the Garden of Gethsemane. Mark 14:51,52 says, "And there followed him a certain young man, having a linen cloth cast about his naked body; and the young men laid hold on him: and he left the linen cloth, and fled from them naked."

Who was this young man? Why was he following Jesus? Why was he naked? Why was he draped in a linen cloth instead of wearing normal clothes? And why was the Holy Spirit so careful to include this unique story in Mark's account of the Gospel? *What is the significance of this event?*

The key to identifying this young man lies in the "linen cloth" he had lightly draped about his body. The particular Greek word that is used for this "linen cloth" is used in only one other event in the New Testament — to depict the "linen cloth" in which the body of Jesus was wrapped for burial (*see* Matthew 27:59, Mark 15:46, and Luke 23:53). Thus, the only reference we have for this kind of cloth in the New Testament is that of a burial shroud used for covering a dead body in the grave.

Some scholars have tried to say this naked young man was Mark himself. They assume that when Mark heard about Jesus' arrest, he quickly jumped out of bed and dashed to the Garden of Gethsemane. But the Garden was remotely located, and no one could have run there so quickly. It is simply a physical impossibility.

Others have speculated that Mark threw off his clothes in an attempt to shock and distract the soldiers so Jesus could escape. This idea is preposterous. Others have tried with similar vain attempts to assert that this naked young man was the apostle John. But why would John be walking naked in the Garden of Gethsemane?

As I said, the answer to this naked young man's identity lies in the cloth he had wrapped around his body. You see, when a body was prepared for burial, it was washed, ceremonially cleaned, and buried naked in a linen cloth exactly like the one described here in the Gospel of Mark. Furthermore, the Garden of Gethsemane was situated on the side of the Mount of Olives. Toward the base of that mount is a heavily populated cemetery, with many of its graves going back to the time of Jesus.

When Jesus said, "I AM," the power released was so tremendous that it knocked the soldiers backward. But evidently, it also caused a rumbling in the local cemetery! When that blast of power was released, a young boy, draped in a linen burial cloth in accordance with the tradition of that time, crawled out from his tomb — *raised from the dead*!

The reason he "followed" Jesus was to get a glimpse of the One who had resurrected him. The word "followed" here means *to continuously follow*. This tells us that this resurrected young man trailed the soldiers as they took Jesus through the Garden on the way to His trial. When the soldiers discovered the young man who was following Jesus, they tried to apprehend him. But when they reached out to grab him, he broke free from their grip and fled, leaving the linen cloth in their possession.

I want you to reflect again on the amazing power that was active at the time of Jesus' arrest in the Garden of Gethsemane. He later told

Pilate, "…Thou couldest have no power at all against me, except it were given thee from above…" (John 19:11). Indeed, there was so much power present that *no one* could have withstood Jesus had He chosen to resist. Jesus was not taken by the will of man; He was delivered by the will of the Father.

The only reason Jesus was taken was that He chose to willingly lay down His life for you and for me.

Think how marvelous it is that Jesus freely gave His life for us! So much power was at work in Him, even at the time of His arrest, that no one had sufficient power to forcibly take Him. The only reason Jesus could be taken was that He chose to willingly lay down His life for you and for me.

Don't read these words lightly. Allow the magnitude of what Jesus did for you to sink deep into your heart. Take some time to stop and thank Him for being so willing to go to the Cross and to bear the punishment for your sin in your stead. Jesus is worthy of your heartfelt praise!

Think About It

When Jesus simply acknowledged who He was, the blast of power released in that truth not only knocked His enemies backward, but it also raised the dead.

Consider what will happen in your life when you, with conviction, acknowledge who Jesus is on your behalf. In what areas do you need to acknowledge Him the most?

The divine power available to Jesus that night in the Garden is unfathomable to our natural minds. Yet He chose not to resist the soldiers; instead, in obedience He yielded to the will of God.

Meditate on the great love and self-sacrifice Jesus displayed in choosing to give His life for you. In what ways can you begin to yield your life to Him more fully and to follow His leading more accurately as you walk through each day?

No foe could have withstood the power in Jesus if He had chosen to resist His enemies. If *you* resist the devil, he cannot withstand the power of God that resides in *you*.

Consider some areas in your life where the devil is seeking to overtake you. Then take the time to think about the overwhelming power of the Greater One within you. Make a quality decision to submit to God in every area of your life, and then use your authority in Jesus' name to actively *resist* the enemy!

14

A Holy Life
Laid Down for You

chapter

14

A Holy Life
Laid Down for You

After Jesus demonstrated His phenomenal power, He permitted the soldiers to take Him into custody. In a certain sense, this was simply an *act*, for He'd already vividly proven that they didn't have adequate power to take Him. Just one word and He had put the soldiers on their backs — yet the Bible says, "And they that *had laid hold on Jesus led him away* to Caiaphas the high priest, where the scribes and the elders were assembled" (Matthew 26:57).

The words "laid hold" are from the Greek word *kratos*. In this case, this word means *to seize, to take hold of, to firmly grip*, or *to apprehend*. Used in this context, it primarily carries the idea of *making a forceful arrest*. Once Jesus demonstrated that He could not be taken by force, He then allowed the soldiers to seize Him.

Matthew 26:57 goes on to tell us that once Jesus was in their hands, they "led him away." This phrase comes from the Greek word *apago* — the same word used to picture *a shepherd who ties a rope around the neck of his sheep and then leads it down the path to where it needs to go.*

This word depicts exactly what happened to Jesus that night in the Garden of Gethsemane. He wasn't gagged and dragged to the high priest as one who was putting up a fight or resisting arrest. Instead, the Greek word *apago* plainly tells us that the soldiers lightly slipped a rope about Jesus' neck and led Him down the path as He followed behind, just like a sheep being led by a shepherd. Thus, the Roman soldiers and temple police led Him as a sheep to slaughter, just as Isaiah 53:7 had prophesied many centuries earlier. Specifically on that night, however, the soldiers led Jesus to Caiaphas, the high priest.

Let's see what we can learn about Caiaphas. We know that Caiaphas was appointed high priest in the year 18 AD. As high priest, he became so prominent in Israel that even when his term as high priest ended, he wielded great influence in the business of the nation, including its spiritual, political, and financial affairs. Flavius Josephus, the famous Jewish historian, reported that five of Caiaphas' sons later served in the office of the high priest.[2]

As a young man, Caiaphas married Anna, the daughter of Annas, who was serving as high priest at that time. Annas served as Israel's high priest for nine years. The title of high priest had fallen into the jurisdiction of this family, and they held this high-ranking position firmly in their grip, passing it among the various members of the family and thus keeping the reins of power in their hands. It was a spiritual monarchy. The holders of this coveted title retained great political power, controlled public opinion, and owned vast wealth.

After Annas was removed by the Romans, the title of high priest passed to his son-in-law Caiaphas. Annas continued to exercise control over the nation through his son-in-law. This influence is evident in Luke 3:2, where the Bible says, "Annas and Caiaphas being the high priests...." It was impossible for two people to serve as high priests at the same time; nonetheless, Annas held his former title and much of his former authority. He was so influential at the very end of Jesus' ministry that the Roman soldiers and temple police who arrested Jesus in the Garden of Gethsemane led Jesus to Annas first before delivering him to Caiaphas, the current high priest (John 18:13).

Both Annas and Caiaphas were Sadducees, a group of religious leaders who were more liberal in doctrine and had a tendency not to believe in supernatural events. In fact, they regarded most supernatural occurrences in the Old Testament as myths.[3]

The constant reports of Jesus' supernatural powers and miracles, as well as the reputation He was gaining throughout the nation, caused Caiaphas, Annas, and the other members of the Sanhedrin to view Jesus as a threat. These religious leaders were control freaks in the truest sense of the words, and it was an affront to them that Jesus' ministry was beyond their control and jurisdiction. Then they heard the verified report that Lazarus had actually been resurrected from the dead! This incident drove them over the edge, causing them to decide to murder Jesus.

These leaders were so filled with rage about Lazarus' resurrection and were so worried about Jesus' growing popularity that they held a secret council to determine whether or not Jesus had to be killed. Once that decision was made, Caiaphas was the one who was principally responsible for scheming how to bring His death to pass.

As high priest and the official head of the Sanhedrin, Caiaphas was also responsible for arranging Jesus' illegal trial before the Jewish authorities. At first, he charged Jesus with the sin of blasphemy. However, because Jesus wouldn't contest the accusation Caiaphas brought against Him, the high priest then delivered Him to the Roman authorities, who found Jesus guilty of treason for claiming to be the king of the Jews.

Caiaphas was so powerful that even after the death of Jesus, he continued to persecute believers in the Early Church. For instance, after the crippled man at the Beautiful Gate was healed (see Acts 3), Peter and John were seized and brought before the council (Acts 4:6). Caiaphas was the high priest at this time and continued to serve as high priest until he was removed in 36 AD.

This emphatically tells us that Caiaphas was also the high priest who interrogated Stephen in Acts 7:1. In addition, he was the high priest we read about who gave Saul of Tarsus written permission that authorized him to arrest believers in Jerusalem and later in Damascus (Acts 9:1,2).

Because of the political events in the year 36 AD, Caiaphas was finally removed from the office of high priest. Of the 19 men who served as high priests in the first century, this evil man ruled the longest. The title of high priest, however, remained in the family after Caiaphas stepped down, this time passed on to his brother-in-law Jonathan, another son of Annas.

Consider this: Jesus had never sinned (2 Corinthians 5:21); no guile had ever been found in His mouth (1 Peter 2:22); and His entire life was devoted to doing good and to healing all who were oppressed of the devil (Acts 10:38). Therefore, it seems entirely unjust that He would be led like a sheep into the midst of the spiritual vipers who were ruling in Jerusalem. According to the flesh, one could have argued that this wasn't fair. However, Jesus never questioned the Father's will or balked at the assignment that was required of Him.

The apostle Peter wrote this regarding Jesus: "Who, when he was reviled, reviled not again; when he suffered, he threatened not; but committed himself to him that judgeth righteously" (1 Peter 2:23). The word "committed" is the Greek word *paradidomi*, a compound of the words *para* and *didomi*. The word *para* means *alongside* and carries the idea of *coming close alongside to someone or to some object*. The word *didomi* means *to give*. When these two words are compounded together, the new word presents the idea of *entrusting something to someone*. The prefix *para* suggests that this is someone to whom you have drawn *very close*. It can be translated *to commit, to yield, to commend, to transmit, to deliver*, or *to hand something over to someone else*.

Knowing He was in the Father's will, the Lord Jesus yielded Himself to the One who judges righteously when He found Himself in this unjust situation. In that difficult hour, Jesus drew close to the Father, fully entrusting Himself and His future into His Father's hands and leaving the results in His control.

If you are in a situation that seems unfair or unjust and there is nothing you can do to change it, you must draw as close to the Father as

In that difficult hour, Jesus drew close to the Father, fully entrusting Himself and His future into His Father's hands.

you can and commit yourself into His loving care. You know He wants the best for you, even though you have found yourself in a predicament that seems so undeserved. Your options are to get angry and bitter and turn sour toward life, or to choose to believe that God is in control and working on your behalf, even if you don't see anything good happening at the present moment.

When Jesus was arrested and taken to Caiaphas to be severely mistreated, there was no escape for Him. He had no choice but to trust the Father.

What other choice do *you* have today?

Think About It

God is love, and Jesus personified that love as He walked on the earth. The cruelty and unbridled hatred Jesus experienced at the hands of corrupt religious leaders was insane and unjust. Yet through it all, He drew close to the Father, entrusting the final outcome into His Father's hands.

When you have faced injustice in the past, did you fully entrust your heart, your circumstances, and your final outcome to the Father? How can you trust Him more? Think about it.

Life is not always fair. At times there is nothing you can do to change a situation; all you can do is walk through it. In those moments, you must remind yourself that your Father God is greater than all. He has a plan for you, to give you a hope and a future (Jeremiah 29:11).

Are you or someone you love in an undeserved predicament? What can you do to release the matter into the hands of God? How can you express your commitment to put your trust in God and not in man?

When Jesus was taken to be severely mistreated, there seemed to be no means of escape for Him. Evil men thought they had Him in their power; however, a *higher* purpose was at work.

When evil appears to prevail and you seem to have no way out, one freedom remains: *You can still choose how you will respond.* Your options? You can either become angry with people and grow bitterly resentful, or you can draw near to God and rest your heart upon His faithfulness as you simply trust in Him. The choice is yours. Carefully consider the consequences of your options, and then determine your response.

chapter

15

Has Anyone Ever Spit in Your Face?

chapter

15

Has Anyone Ever Spit in Your Face?

Some years ago, I visited another church in our city to hear a special speaker who had come from afar. That evening at the meeting, the local church I was visiting announced they would be starting a building program. As I sat there, God's Spirit spoke to my heart and instructed me to sow a sacrificial seed into their new building program. It was a time when we desperately needed money for our own building program, so *anything* I sowed would have been a sacrifice. However, the amount the Lord put in my heart was significantly beyond what my natural mind would have possibly conceived.

What made it even harder for me to give this gift was that this church had acted maliciously toward our church in the past. They had lied about us, scoffed at us, and even prayed for our downfall. *And now the Lord was telling me to sow a large gift into this same church?*

Throughout that entire service, I argued with the Lord. The issue really wasn't the money, although we could have used the money ourselves at that moment. The issue I was wrestling with was giving a gift to this church that had treated us with contempt for so long.

Finally, the Spirit of God asked me, *Are you willing to sow a seed for peace with this church?* That clinched it! I pulled my checkbook out of my pocket to write what I considered to be a sizable gift for this or any other church. Writing that check was difficult, but once it was written, my heart simply flooded with joy because I had been obedient. There is no joy to compare with that which comes from being obedient!

One week later, the pastor to whom I gave the gift was at a meeting with his staff and church leaders. The pastor told his leaders, "Look at this puny little check Pastor Rick gave us! Couldn't he have done any better than this?"

When I heard how this pastor viewed the financial gift I'd given, I was quite shocked. But I was literally stunned by what this pastor did next. He devoted the next part of his staff meeting to discussing all the things he didn't like about our church and about me. He poked fun at us, ridiculed us, mocked us, and put us down in front of his people. Instead of being thankful for the gift we gave, he once again demonstrated utter disrespect and contempt for us.

When I heard about this event, it hurt so badly that it cut deep into my heart. How could anyone say the gift we gave was puny? It would be considered significant in any nation of the world. But what hurt the most was that the pastor had put us down and publicly made fun of us in front of his staff and leadership. I remember feeling as if I had been spit on — and as the years passed, this same pastor spit on us many more times.

For instance, when we dedicated our church building — the first church to be built in 60 years in our city — it was a moment of great rejoicing. But soon after our dedication, this man stood before a large convention of several thousand people and sneered at our new facility. For a second time, he injected a dagger into my heart! At a time when this pastor could have been rejoicing with us, he chose to make it another opportunity to spit in our faces.

How about you? Can you think of an instance in your life when you did something good for someone, but that person didn't appreciate what you did? Was he so unappreciative that you felt as if he'd spit in your face? Were you stunned by his behavior? How did you act in response to that situation?

I think nearly everyone has felt taken advantage of and spit on at some point or another. But imagine how Jesus must have felt the night He was taken to the high priest where He was *literally* spit on by the guards and temple police! For three years, Jesus preached, taught, and healed the sick. But now He was being led like a sheep to the spiritual butcher of Jerusalem, the high priest Caiaphas, and to the scribes and elders who had assembled to wait for His arrival.

In the trial that took place before the high priest and his elders, the religious leaders charged Jesus with the crime of declaring Himself the Messiah. Jesus replied by telling them that they would indeed one day see Him sitting on the right hand of power and coming with clouds of glory (Matthew 26:64). Upon hearing this, the high priest ripped his clothes and screamed, *"Blasphemy!"* as all the scribes and elders lifted their voices in anger, demanding that Jesus would suffer the penalty of *death* (Matthew 26:66).

Then these religious scribes and elders did the *unthinkable*! Matthew 26:67,68 says, "Then did they spit in his face, and buffeted him; and others smote him with the palms of their hands, saying, Prophesy unto us, thou Christ, Who is he that smote thee?"

Notice that it wasn't just a few who spit in His face that night. The Bible says, "...*they* spit in his face...." The word "they" refers to all the scribes and elders who were assembled for the meeting that night. One scholar notes that there could have been 100 or more men in this crowd! And one by one, each of these so-called spiritual leaders, clothed in their religious garments, walked up to Jesus and spit in His face!

In that culture and time, spitting in someone's face was considered to be the strongest thing you could do to show utter disgust, repugnance, dislike, or hatred. When someone spattered his spit on another person's face, that spit was meant to humiliate, demean, debase, and shame that person. To make it worse, the offender would usually spit hard and close to the person's face, making it all the more humiliating.

By the time Caiaphas and his scribes and elders had finished taking turns spitting on Jesus, their spit was most likely dripping down from His forehead into His eyes; dribbling down His nose, His cheekbones, and His chin; and even oozing down onto His clothes. This was an extremely humiliating scene! And remember, the men who were acting so hatefully toward Jesus were religious leaders! Their hideous conduct was something Jesus definitely didn't deserve. And what makes this entire scene even more amazing is that Malchus — the servant whom Jesus had just healed — was in all probability standing at the side of Caiaphas and watching it all happen!

These religious leaders didn't stop with just humiliating Jesus. After spitting on Him, they each doubled up their fists and hit Him violently in the face! Matthew 26:67 says, "Then did they spit in his face, *and buffeted him....*" The word "buffet" is the Greek word *kolaphidzo*, which means *to strike with the fist.* It is normally used to picture a person who is *violently beaten.*

As if it wasn't insulting enough to spit on Jesus, approximately 100 men viciously and cruelly struck Him with their fists. Not only was this brutal — it was sadistic! Humiliating Jesus with their spit and curses didn't satisfy the hatred of these men; they wouldn't be satisfied until they knew He had been physically maltreated. To ensure that this goal was accomplished, their own fists became their weapons of abuse.

It appears that these scribes and elders were so paranoid about Jesus getting more attention than themselves that they simply wanted to destroy Him. Every time they spit on Him, they were spitting on the anointing. Every time they struck Him, they were leveling a punch against the anointing. They hated Jesus and the anointing that operated through Him to such an extent that they voted to murder Him. But first they wanted to take some time to personally make sure He suffered before He died. What a strange way to render "thanks" to One who had done so much for them!

When I get disappointed at the way others respond to me or to what I have done for them, I often think of what happened to Jesus on that night when He came before these Jewish leaders. John 1:11 tells us, "He came unto his own, and his own received him not." Although these men who spit on and hit Jesus refused to acknowledge Him, He still went to the Cross and died for them. His love for them was unwavering — unshaken and unaffected by their wrong actions.

Although these men who spit on and hit Jesus refused to acknowledge Him, He still went to the Cross and died for them. His love for them was unwavering — unshaken and unaffected by their wrong actions.

When you think about the way people have wronged you in the past, does it affect your desire to love them? What have these conflicts revealed about *you*? Is your love for those unkind people consistent, unwavering, unshaken, and unaffected? Or have the conflicts revealed that you have a fickle love, which you quickly turn off when people don't respond to you the way you wished they would?

The same Holy Spirit who lived in Jesus now lives in you. Just as the Spirit of God empowered Jesus to love people consistently, regardless of what they did or didn't do, the Holy Spirit can empower you to do the same.

It is your responsibility to walk as Jesus walked regarding those who have let you down or disappointed you in your life. So take a few minutes right now to identify the individuals who fit this description. Then I encourage you to *pray* for them. Forgive each person, one by one, and then release them from their sin against you. Make the choice to follow your Master's example, loving those who have wronged you the way Jesus loved those who so grievously wronged Him.

Think About It

When you give a gift with sincere motives, it is surprising and hurtful to have the recipient express disdain for the gift or disrespect toward you as the giver. Has someone ever made light of a gift that you gave with the intention of blessing him or her? How did you feel?

Imagine how Jesus felt, knowing that He was giving His life for people who not only mocked His purpose, but also wanted Him to suffer and feel humiliated even as He gave to them. Think about the depth of love and humility Jesus walked in — just for you.

What kinds of attitudes and actions serve as a "spit in the face" toward another individual? Have you ever demonstrated those attitudes and actions toward God concerning His gifts to you? Think about it.

Disrespect and dishonor are far too easy to find in our modern society. On the other hand, honor, respect, and appreciation are rare, yet so very valuable. How can you build more honor and appreciation into your responses to others? What positive influence can you have in the life of someone you know, simply by displaying honor toward him or her — particularly if that person has been dishonored by others?

chapter

16

Playing Games at Jesus' Expense

chapter

16

Playing Games at Jesus' Expense

If we're going to get the full picture of what happened in Caiaphas' chamber that night when the religious leaders were spitting on Jesus and striking Him in the face with their fists, we need to pull all the pieces of this picture together from the Gospels of both Matthew and Luke.

Luke 22:63 says, "And the men that held Jesus mocked him, and smote him." I want you to particularly see the word "mock" in this verse. It comes from the Greek word *empaidzo*, which meant *to play a game*. It was often used for *playing a game with children* or for *amusing a crowd by impersonating someone in a silly and exaggerated way*. For instance, this word might be used in a game of charades when someone intends to *comically portray someone or even make fun of someone*. This gives us an important piece of the story that Matthew didn't include in his Gospel account.

Even before He had to endure the spitting and vicious beating of the scribes and elders that night, Jesus was also severely beaten by "the men that held" Him. This doesn't refer to the scribes and elders, but to the temple police and guards who kept watch over Jesus before Caiaphas examined Him.

In addition to everything else that was going on that night, these guards decided they would take advantage of the moment too. The Bible doesn't tell us how these men mimicked and impersonated Jesus that night, but the use of the Greek word *empaidzo* categorically lets us know that these men turned a few minutes of that nightmarish night into a stage of comedy at Jesus' expense. They put on quite a show, hamming it up as they almost certainly pretended to be Jesus and the people He ministered to. Perhaps they laid hands on each other as if they were healing the sick; or lay on the floor and quivered, as if they were being liberated from devils; or wobbled around, acting as if they had been blind but now could suddenly see. Whatever these guards did to mock Jesus, it was a game of charades to mimic and make fun of Him.

When they were finished making sport of Jesus, Luke tells us that these guards "smote him." The word for "smote" is from the word *dero*, a word used frequently to refer to *the grueling and barbaric practice of beating a slave*. This word is so dreadful that it is also often translated *to flay*, such as *to flay the flesh from an animal or human being*. The usage of this word tells us that even before the scribes and elders got their hands on Jesus, the guards had already put Him through a terrible ordeal.

Immediately after the guards finished playing their charades and brutally beating Jesus, the scribes and elders began to spit in His face and pummel Him on the head with their fists. But the elders didn't stop there. They blindfolded Jesus and began to strike Him on the head *again*, taking their humiliation of Him to the next level. This was Jesus' third beating.

If we read only Luke's account, we might conclude that this third beating was also at the hands of the guards. However, when we compare and connect Luke's account with Matthew's account, it becomes clear that by this time Jesus had already been transferred into the hands of Caiaphas and his scribes and elders. What we read next in Luke 22:64 occurred *after* these religious leaders had already spit on Him and hit Him (Matthew 26:67).

Luke 22:64 says, "And when they had blindfolded him, they struck him on the face, and asked him, saying, Prophesy, who is it that smote thee?" The word "blindfolded" comes from the Greek word *perikalupto*, which means *to wrap a veil or garment about someone, thus hiding his eyes so he can't see*. We don't know where the blindfold came from. It could have been a piece of Jesus' own clothing or a garment borrowed from one of the scribes and elders. But by the time they finished wrapping Jesus' head in that cloth, He was completely blinded from seeing what was happening around him.

Just as the guards played *charades* at Jesus' expense, now Caiaphas with the scribes and elders did the same with *blind man's bluff*! Once Jesus was blindfolded, "they *struck* him on the face." The word "struck" is from the Greek word *paio*, which describes *a strike that stings*. A more precise translation might be *"they slapped him on the face."* This is the reason the Greek word *paio* was used, for it referred to *a slap that causes a terrible sting*.

After slapping Jesus, the scribes and elders would badger Him, saying, "...Prophesy, who is it that smote thee?" Here we find that these so-called religious leaders became so caught up in their sick behavior that they sadistically enjoyed the pain they were putting Jesus through. They slapped Him over and again, telling Him, *"Come on, prophet! If You're so good at prophesying and knowing things supernaturally, tell us which one of us just slapped You!"*

Finally, Luke 22:65 tells us, "And many other things blasphemously spake they against him." The word "blasphemy" is from the Greek word *blasphemeo*, meaning *to slander*; *to accuse*; *to speak against*; or *to speak derogatory words for the purpose of injuring or harming one's reputation*. It also signifies *profane, foul, unclean language*.

When Luke says they "blasphemously spake," he is talking about Caiaphas with his scribes and elders! Once these religious leaders "took off the lid," every foul thing that was hiding inside them came to the top. It was as if a monster had been let out, and they couldn't get it back in its cage!

Jesus had told these religious leaders earlier, "Woe unto you, scribes and Pharisees, hypocrites! for ye are like unto whited sepulchres, which indeed appear beautiful outward, but are within full of dead men's bones, and of all uncleaness" (Matthew 23:27). In the end, the death and uncleanness in their souls came raging to the top as they screamed and yelled at Jesus using profane, foul, unclean language.

I'm sure that if the people of Israel had been allowed to sneak a peek into that room that night, they would have been horrified to see their supposedly godly leaders slapping Jesus, spitting on Him, slapping Him again, and then screaming curses right in His face! Here these leaders were — all dressed up in their religious garb, but inwardly so rotten that they could not hide their true nature anymore.

So let me ask you two questions:

1. Are you serious in your relationship with Jesus Christ — or are you, like those who held Him that night, simply playing games with Him?

2. When other people start playing around with *your* mind and emotions, are you able to follow Jesus' example by holding your peace and loving them in spite of the torment they are putting you through?

Let's covenant together from this day forward to never be like the backslidden religious leaders in this story. How terrible it is to outwardly look beautiful but to inwardly be so ugly! To avoid this scenario in our own lives, we must make the commitment to be serious in our relationship with Jesus and absolutely *refuse* to play games with God.

And should you ever find yourself in a predicament similar to the one Jesus faced — in other words, if people are emotionally abusing you or taking advantage of you — call out to God to strengthen you! He will give you the wisdom to know when you should speak, when you should be quiet, and exactly what steps you must take. When you find yourself in this kind of tight place, just be certain to guard your mouth and let the

Holy Spirit dictate your emotions so you can demonstrate the love of God to those whom the devil is trying to use against you.

Jesus is the perfect Example of the way we must behave in all situations. Although He was blasphemed, reviled, and cursed, He never fought back or allowed Himself to be dragged into a war of words. For this reason, Peter exhorted us to follow in Jesus' steps: "For even hereunto were ye called: because Christ also suffered for us, leaving us an example, that ye should follow his steps: who did no sin, neither was guile found in his mouth" (1 Peter 2:21,22).

Although Jesus was blasphemed, reviled, and cursed, He never fought back or allowed Himself to be dragged into a war of words.

Today you can make the decision to come up to a higher level in your commitment to Jesus Christ. You can refuse to play games with God or to deceive yourself any longer about your own spiritual condition. The truth about what is in you will eventually come out anyway, so take an honest look at your soul now to make sure there are no hidden flaws that will later come rising up to the surface.

Open your heart, and allow the Holy Spirit to shine His glorious light into the crevices of your soul. Allow Him to reveal those areas of your life where you need to yield to His cleansing work. As you do, you will find yourself becoming more and more transformed into the image of Jesus, who left you an example so you could follow in His steps.

Think About It

Mental and emotional abuse at the hands of others is devastatingly cruel. Such deliberately focused mocking and humiliation can leave horrible emotional scars. Jesus endured this kind of torture from His enemies, in addition to unthinkable, sadistic physical abuse.

If you are in a similar predicament — if people are emotionally abusing you — call out to God! Not only will He strengthen you, but He will also give you the wisdom you need concerning the steps you must take.

Jesus told the scribes and religious leaders that they were like beautiful tombs — lovely to look upon, but full of filth and uncleanness. They verified His words with their profane, vulgar language and vicious behavior toward Jesus.

Are there any areas of your life that look lovely to others, yet are hiding motives and behavior that are unclean? Are you deceiving yourself and playing games at Jesus' expense? Take an honest look at your own life. What is in you will eventually come out for all to see. Think about it.

Our flesh always wants to retaliate when we've been wronged, but Jesus gave us the perfect example to follow. When He was cursed, He refused to be dragged down to the level of His attackers. No guile was found in His mouth.

How can you pattern your responses to wrong treatment to be more in line with Jesus' responses? What inward and outward adjustments can you make in your own life?

chapter

17

*Surrender and Release
Yourself Into the Loving
Care of God*

chapter

17

Surrender and Release Yourself Into the Loving Care of God

Have you ever found yourself in a situation where you felt like you were surrounded and besieged by control freaks who were obsessed with keeping everything that moved under their monitoring direction? If you've been in a situation like this before, you know how hard it is to function in that kind of environment.

Well, at the time of Jesus' ministry on earth, Israel was overwhelmed with scads of leaders who were obsessed with the notion of holding on to the reins of power. This paranoia was so epidemic that it had spread to both the religious and political world. The high priest, along with his scribes and elders, were suspicious and paranoid of anyone who appeared to be growing in popularity. The political leaders installed by Rome to preside over Israel were just as paranoid, looking behind every nook and cranny for opponents and constantly struggling to keep power in their grip.

Israel was under the enemy control of Rome, an occupying force that the Jews despised. They hated the Romans for their pagan tendencies, for pushing the Roman language and culture on them, and for the taxes they were required to pay to Rome. And that's just a few of the reasons the Jews hated the Romans.

Because of the political turmoil in Israel, few political leaders from Rome held power for very long, and those who succeeded did so using cruelty and brutality. The land was full of revolts, rebellions, insurgencies, assassinations, and endless political upheavals. The ability to rule long in this environment required a ruthless, self-concerned leader who was willing to do anything necessary to maintain a position of power. This leads us to *Pontius Pilate*, who was just that type of man.

After Herod Archelaus was removed from power (*see* chapter 19 to find out more about the three sons of Herod the Great), Judea was placed in the care of a Roman procurator. This was a natural course of events, for the Roman Empire was already divided into approximately 40 provinces, each governed by a procurator — a position that was the equivalent of a *governor*.

It was normal for a procurator to serve in his position for 12 to 36 months. However, Pilate governed Judea for ten years, beginning in the year 26 AD and concluding in the year 36 AD. This ten-year span of time is critical, for it means Pilate was governor of Judea throughout the entire length of Jesus' ministry. The Jewish historian, Flavius Josephus, noted that Pilate was ruthless and unsympathetic and that he failed to comprehend and appreciate how important the Jews' religious beliefs and convictions were to them.

In addition to the normal responsibilities a procurator possessed, Pilate also ruled as the supreme authority in legal matters. An expert in Roman law, he had the final say-so in nearly all the legal decisions for the territory of Judea. However, even though Pilate held this awesome legal power in his hands, he dreaded cases having to do with religion and often permitted such cases to be passed into the court of the Sanhedrin, over which Caiaphas the high priest presided.

Pilate lived at Herod's palace, located in Caesarea. Because it was the official residence of the procurator, a military force of about 3,000 Roman soldiers was stationed there to protect the Roman governor. Pilate disliked the city of Jerusalem and recoiled from making visits there. But at the time of the feasts when the city of Jerusalem was filled with guests, travelers, and strangers, there was a greater potential of unrest, turbulence, and disorder, so Pilate and his troops would come into the city of Jerusalem to guard and protect the peace of the population. This was the reason Pilate was in the city of Jerusalem at the time of Jesus' crucifixion.

As a highly political man, Pilate knew how to play the political game — as did the Jews he ruled. In fact, so many complaints had been filed in Rome about Pilate's unkind and ruthless style of ruling that the threat of an additional complaint was often all that was needed for the Jews to manipulate Pilate to do their bidding. This no doubt affected Pilate's decision to crucify Jesus.

That day the high priest, the Sanhedrin, and the entire mob insisted that Jesus be crucified. Pilate wanted to know the reason for this demand, so they answered him, "…We found this fellow perverting the nation, and forbidding to give tribute to Caesar, saying that he himself is Christ a King" (Luke 23:2).

Pilate knew the Jews were jealous of Jesus. But politically the charges they brought against Jesus put him in a very bad position. What if the news reached Rome that Jesus had perverted the nation, teaching the people to withhold their taxes and claiming to be a counter King in place of the Roman emperor? It would be political suicide for Pilate to do nothing about that kind of situation. The Jewish leaders were well aware of this when they fabricated these charges against Jesus. They knew exactly what political strings to pull to get Pilate to do what they wanted — and they were pulling every string they held in their hands.

The Jewish people loathed Pilate for his cruelty and inadequate care of his subjects. The kind of brutality that made him so infamous and so hated can be seen in Luke 13:1, where it mentions that Pilate slaughtered a number of Galileans and then mixed their blood together with the sacrifices. As appalling and sick as this act may sound, it is in accordance with many other vicious actions instigated under Pilate's rule as procurator of Judea.

Another example of Pilate's callousness can be seen in an incident that occurred when a prophet claimed to possess a supernatural gift that enabled him to locate consecrated vessels, which he alleged had been secretly hidden by Moses. When this prophet announced that he would unearth these vessels, Samaritans turned out in large numbers to observe the event. Pilate, who thought the entire affair was a disguise for some other political or military activity, dispatched Roman forces to assault and massacre the crowd that had gathered. In the end, it became apparent that nothing political had been intended.[4]

The Samaritans felt such great loss for those who died that they formally requested the governor of Syria to intervene in this case. Their complaints regarding Pilate became so numerous that Pilate was eventually summoned to Rome to give account for his actions before the Emperor Tiberius himself. But before Pilate could reach Rome to counter the charges that were brought against him, the Emperor Tiberius died.

Outside the Gospels, Pilate is not mentioned again in the New Testament. Historical records show that the procurator of Syria brought some sort of accusations against Pilate in the year 36 AD. These indictments resulted in his removal from office and exile to Gaul (modern-day France). Eusebius, the well-known early Christian historian, later wrote that Pilate fell into misfortune under the wicked Emperor Caligula and lost many privileges. According to Eusebius, this man Pilate — who had ruled Judea ruthlessly and mercilessly for ten years and who was ultimately responsible for the trial, judgment, crucifixion, and burial of Jesus — finally committed suicide.

With this history now behind us, let's look at Matthew 27:2. It says regarding Jesus, "And when they had bound him, they led him away, and delivered him to Pontius Pilate the governor." The word "bound" is the Greek word *desantes*, from the word *deo*, which is the same word that would be used to describe *the binding, tying up, or securing of an animal*. I am confident that this was precisely the connotation Matthew had in mind, for the next phrase uses a word that was common in the world of animal caretakers.

The verse tells us that they "led him away." These words come from the Greek word *apago*. The word *apago* is used for *a shepherd who ties a rope around the neck of his sheep and then leads it down the path to where it needs to go*. Just as the soldiers had led Jesus to Caiaphas, they now slipped a rope about His neck and walked the Lamb of God to Pontius Pilate.

The Bible says that once Jesus was in Pilate's jurisdiction, they then "…delivered him to Pontius Pilate the governor." The word "delivered" is the word *paradidomi*, the same word we saw when Jesus *committed* Himself to the Father who judges righteously. However, in this case, the meaning would more likely be *to commit, to yield, to transmit, to deliver*, or *to hand something over to someone else*.

This means that when the high priest ordered Jesus to be taken to Pilate, he officially made the issue Pilate's problem. The high priest took Jesus to Pilate, delivered Him fully into Pilate's hands, and then left Pilate with the responsibility of finding Him guilty and crucifying Him.

Matthew 27:11 says, "And Jesus stood before the governor: and the governor asked him, saying, Art thou the King of the Jews? And Jesus said unto him, Thou sayest." Pilate asked a direct question, but Jesus refused to directly answer him. Matthew 27:12 goes on to say, "And when he was accused of the chief priests and elders, he answered nothing." So for a second time, Jesus refused to answer or refute the charges that were brought up against Him.

Matthew 27:13,14 tells us what happened next: "Then said Pilate unto him, Hearest thou not how many things they witness against thee? And he answered him to never a word; insomuch that the governor marvelled greatly." Notice the Bible says Pilate "marveled greatly" at Jesus' silence. In Greek, this phrase is the word *thaumadzo*, which means *to wonder; to be at a loss of words*; or *to be shocked and amazed*.

Pilate was dumbfounded by Jesus' silence because Roman law permitted prisoners three chances to open their mouths to defend themselves. If a prisoner passed up those three chances to speak in his defense, he would be automatically charged as "guilty." In Matthew 27:11, Jesus passed up His *first chance*. In Matthew 27:12, He passed up His *second chance*. Now in Matthew 27:14, Jesus passes up His *final chance* to defend Himself.

At the very end of this time of interrogation, Pilate asked Jesus, "...Art thou the King of the Jews? And he answered him and said, Thou sayest it" (Luke 23:3). John's Gospel tells us that Jesus added, "...My kingdom is not of this world: if my kingdom were of this world, then would my servants fight, that I should not be delivered to the Jews: but now is my kingdom not from hence" (John 18:36). After hearing these answers, "then said Pilate to the chief priests and to the people, I find no fault in this man" (Luke 23:4).

As you will see in the next chapter, Pilate searched diligently for a loophole so he wouldn't have to kill Jesus. John 19:12 says, "And from thenceforth Pilate sought to release him...." But nothing Pilate could do was able to stop the Father's plan from being implemented. Even Jesus passed up His three chances to defend Himself, because He knew that the Cross was a part of His purpose for being sent to earth.

Jesus passed up His three chances to defend Himself, because He knew that the Cross was a part of His purpose for being sent to earth.

When Jesus finally answered Pilate's question, He still didn't defend Himself, knowing it was the appointed time for Him to be slain as the Lamb of God who would take away the sins of the world. But Pilate didn't want to crucify Jesus. In fact, the Roman governor began looking for a loophole — for some way out of putting this Man to death.

But Pilate's search for a way out was in vain; the plan *couldn't* be changed because it was time for the Son of God to offer the permanent sacrifice for sin. As Hebrews 9:12 says, "Neither by the blood of goats and calves, but by his own blood he entered in once into the holy place, having obtained eternal redemption for us."

Are you certain of God's plan for your life? Consider whether or not you are able to say with conviction: "I know what God has called me to do, and I'm willing to go where He tells me to go and pay any price I have to pay. My greatest priority and obsession is to do the will of the Father!" If you are *not* able to say this yet, ask the Holy Spirit to help you grow to the point where doing God's will, regardless of the cost, becomes the most important thing in your life. Even if the life of obedience takes you through hard places as it did with Jesus, the end result will be resurrection and victory!

Think About It

Notice that Jesus never responded to Pilate until Pilate presumed to hold power over Jesus' life. In that presumption, Pilate exalted himself above God, in whose hands Jesus had entrusted His life. Jesus corrected Pilate's error, not tolerating any attempt to usurp His Father's true and final authority.

When others attempt to intimidate, control, and manipulate your life or circumstances, remind yourself that your times are in *God's* hands — not man's (Psalm 31:15). If someone is trying to wield undue power over your life, look to the way Jesus responded to Pilate. Consider Jesus' example as you look to God for His wisdom in your particular situation.

A life of obedience is never without cost. There will be difficult places where you face the enemy's opposition to God's will being fulfilled in your life. Are you clear about the plan of God for you? If you do not yet know your life's purpose and priority, ask the Person of the Holy Spirit to help you discover God's will for your life and grow to the point where you will do it — no matter the cost.

Jesus felt no need to defend Himself or to cave in under Pilate's interrogation. In the end, Pilate was stunned by the way Jesus stood silent with composure in the face of so much opposition.

When you are fearless, your opposition fears *you* because you're not subject to your enemy's influence or control. Are you surrounded and under attack in this season of your life? What is your focus when you're being opposed? The one you fear is the one who controls you. Do you walk in the fear of God, living each day in reverent awareness of His holy claim on your life? Think about it.

chapter

18

Pilate Looks for a Loophole!

Pilate had never had a problem with causing bloodshed in the past, so it seems strange that he balked at the thought of crucifying Jesus. As governor and the chief legal authority of the land, Pilate had been invested by Rome with the power to decide who would live or die. This Roman governor was infamous for his cold-hearted, insensitive, and cruel style of leadership and had never found it difficult to order the death of a criminal — until now.

There was something inside Pilate that recoiled at the idea of crucifying Jesus. The Bible doesn't state exactly why Pilate didn't want to crucify Him, but it makes one wonder what he saw in Jesus' eyes when he interrogated Him. We do know Pilate was shocked at the manner in which Jesus carried Himself, for Matthew 27:14 tells us that Pilate "marveled greatly" at Jesus.

The Bible doesn't state exactly why Pilate didn't want to crucify Him, but it makes one wonder what he saw in Jesus' eyes when he interrogated Him.

The words "marveled greatly" are from the Greek word *thaumadzo*, which means *to wonder*, *to be at a loss of words*, or *to be shocked and amazed*. Never before had a man like Jesus stood before Pilate, and the governor was obviously disturbed at the thought of murdering Him.

In fact, Pilate was so disturbed that he decided to probe deeper by asking questions. He was looking for a loophole that would enable him to escape this trap the Jews had set both for Jesus and for himself as well. Indeed, the Jewish leaders had carefully schemed a trap with three potential results, all of which would make them very happy. The three-fold purpose of this trap was as follows:

1. **To see Jesus judged by the Roman court, thus ruining His reputation and guaranteeing His crucifixion, while at the same time vindicating themselves in the eyes of the people.**

To ensure that this happened, the Jewish leaders falsified charges that made Jesus appear to be a bona fide political offender. These were the charges: 1) that He had perverted the whole nation — a religious charge that was the responsibility of the Sanhedrin to judge; 2) that He had commanded people not to pay their taxes to Rome; and 3) that He claimed to be king (*see* Luke 23:2). According to Roman law, Jesus should have been crucified for claiming to be king. If these charges were proven true, Pilate was bound by law to crucify Him. If this is what followed, the first purpose of their scheme would have worked.

2. **To see Pilate wiped out and permanently removed from power on the charge that he was unfaithful to the Roman emperor because he would not crucify a man who claimed to be a rival king to the emperor.**

Had Pilate declined to crucify Jesus, this rejection would have given the Jewish leaders the ammunition they needed to prove to Rome that this governor should be removed from power because he was a traitor to the emperor. News would have reached the emperor of Rome that Pilate had permitted a rival king to live, and Pilate would have been charged with treason (*see* John 19:12).

It is interesting that this same charge was brought against Jesus. It was a charge that most assuredly would have led to Pilate's own death or banishment. If Jesus was allowed to go free by the Roman court, the

Jewish leadership would have been thrilled, for then they would have had a legal reason to expel Pilate from their land. Thus, the second purpose of their scheme would have worked.

3.   **To take Jesus back into their own court in the Sanhedrin if Pilate would not crucify Him, where they had the religious authority to stone Him to death for claiming to be the Son of God.**

The truth is, the Jewish leaders never needed to deliver Jesus to Pilate because the court of the Sanhedrin already had the religious authority to kill Jesus by stoning for claiming to be the Son of God. Even if Pilate refused to crucify Jesus, they fully intended to kill Him anyway (*see* John 19:7).

So we see that the trip to Pilate's court of law was designed to turn Jesus' arrest into a political catastrophe that would possibly help the Jewish leaders get rid of Pilate as well. But if Jesus had been freed by the Roman court, they intended to kill Him anyway. This was the third part of their scheme.

The solution to this mess was easy! All Pilate had to do was crucify Jesus. Then he would have happy Jewish elders on his hands; no charges of treason leveled against him in Rome; strengthened ties to the religious community; and a guarantee of remaining in power. Pilate just had to say, "CRUCIFY HIM!" and this political game would be over. But he couldn't bring himself to utter those words!

Instead, Pilate gave Jesus three opportunities to speak up in His own defense. But Jesus said nothing. Isaiah 53:7 (*NKJV*) says, "...As a sheep before its shearers is silent, so He opened not His mouth." According to the law, Jesus should have automatically been declared "guilty" because He passed up His three chances to defend Himself. But this time Pilate simply could not permit himself to follow the due course of judicial process. He sought instead to find a way out of this dilemma.

As noted above, perhaps Pilate saw something in Jesus' eyes that affected him. Maybe Jesus' kind and gracious behavior grabbed Pilate's heart. Others have speculated that Pilate's wife may have secretly been a follower of Jesus who told her husband about His goodness and the miracles that had followed His life. Matthew 27:19 reports that Pilate's wife was so upset about Jesus' impending death that she even had upsetting dreams about Him in the night. She sent word about her dreams to Pilate, begging him not to crucify Jesus.

As Pilate probed deeper in his interrogation, he discovered that Jesus was from Galilee. At long last, Pilate could breathe a sigh of relief. He had found the loophole that shifted the full weight of the decision to his old enemy, Herod! Galilee was under the legal jurisdiction of Herod. What a coincidence! Herod just "happened" to be in Jerusalem that week to participate in the Feast of Passover!

Pilate promptly ordered Jesus to be transferred to the other side of the city to the residence where Herod was staying with his royal entourage. The Bible tells us, "And when Herod saw Jesus, he was exceeding glad: for he was desirous to see him of a long season, because he had heard many things of him; and he hoped to have seen some miracle done by him" (Luke 23:8). However, it didn't take long for Herod to get angry with Jesus and return Him to Pilate!

Can you imagine what went through Jesus' mind as He stood first before a Roman governor, then before a Jewish tetrarch — only to be shipped back to the Roman governor again? Have *you* been feeling knocked around and passed from one authority figure to another at home, at church, in the workplace, or in the governmental system? If so, you can feel free to talk to Jesus about it, because He really understands the predicament you find yourself in right now!

Hebrews 4:15,16 says, "For we have not an high priest which cannot be touched with the feelings of our infirmities; but was in all points tempted like as we are, yet without sin. Let us therefore come boldly unto the throne of grace, that we may obtain mercy, and find grace to help in time of need." Since Jesus understands your dilemma, I advise you to speak freely to Him about the emotional ups and downs you feel as a result of your situation. His throne is a throne of grace — a place where you can obtain mercy and find grace to help in your time of need.

So go boldly before Jesus' throne, with full assurance that He will hear you, answer you, and give you the power and wisdom you need to press through every difficult situation in your life.

Think About It

Pilate saw through the religious leaders' thinly veiled trap set to destroy both him and Jesus. If Pilate didn't command Jesus to be crucified, he would be considered a traitor to the Roman government. If he did command Jesus to be crucified, Pilate would be a pawn in the Jewish leaders' hands, bearing the blame for accomplishing what they already intended to do.

Have you ever felt caught in a strategic trap of the enemy? When you're faced with that kind of situation, how do you escape such a trap with your integrity intact?

Pilate had ordered the murder of many and wasn't afraid to kill one more. What do you think he saw in Jesus' eyes that disturbed him so greatly? Why do you think Pilate felt compelled to keep probing for a way to defend Jesus and to seek His release?

It's frustrating to endure the negative consequences when a person in authority chooses to shift responsibility to someone else because he or she isn't willing to take a stand and simply do the right thing. Have you ever felt shoved around because someone in authority refused to stand up and speak in your defense when he or she had the opportunity? Jesus felt that way when Pilate shoved Him over to Herod's court.

If you are getting the runaround because someone isn't willing to make a correct judgment call, go boldly before the throne of grace and plead your case before your Father God. He is the Righteous Judge who will surely decree what is right. Have you entrusted yourself to Him, asking Him to perfect that which concerns you?

chapter

19

Herod Meets Jesus!

19

Herod Meets Jesus!

After Pilate discovered Jesus was from Galilee, the jurisdiction of Herod, the Roman governor quickly sent Jesus off to see Herod. At that time, Herod was in Jerusalem to celebrate the Feast of Passover with the Jewish people. But before we get into Herod's excited anticipation to meet Jesus, let's first see which Herod this verse is talking about.

Several men named Herod ruled in Israel over the years. The first and most famous was "Herod the Great," who was made the first governor of Galilee when he was 25 years old. His kingship was launched by the order of Octavius and Marc Antony — the same Marc Antony who had a famous relationship with Cleopatra, the Queen of Egypt. Flavius Josephus, the well-known Jewish historian, recorded that Herod the Great died in 4 BC.

After the death of Herod the Great, his territory was divided among his three sons. These three sons (also named "Herod") were as follows:[5]

HEROD ARCHELAUS

Herod Archelaus was made governor of Samaria, Judea, and Idumea in 4 BC when his father died, and he ruled until approximately 6 AD. This makes him the Herod who was ruling when Mary, Joseph, and Jesus returned from their flight to Egypt (*see* Matthew 2:22).

When Herod Archelaus ascended to the throne in 4 BC, things almost immediately went sour for him. The first problem he confronted was a rebellion incited among Jewish students by their teachers. Because the Ten Commandments forbid graven images, these teachers encouraged their students to tear down and destroy the imperial golden eagle that Rome had ordered to be hung on the entrance to the temple. As punishment, Herod Archelaus ordered these teachers and students to be burned alive. The massacre continued until 3,000 Jews had been slaughtered during the Feast of Passover. Soon Herod Archelaus journeyed to Rome to be crowned by the Emperor Augustus. However, fresh riots ensued in his absence, resulting in more than 2,000 people being crucified.

The Gospel of Matthew indicates that Joseph and Mary were troubled about settling in the territories ruled by Herod Archelaus and therefore made their home in Galilee (Matthew 2:22). Herod Archelaus was so despised that the Jews and Samaritans, usually foes, united together and corporately appealed to Rome to request that he should be removed from power. In 6 AD, Herod Archelaus was banished to Gaul (modern-day France) and died before the year 18.

HEROD PHILIP

Herod Philip was educated in Rome, along with his brothers Herod Archelaus and Herod Antipas. When his father, Herod the Great, died in 4 BC, Herod Philip became governor of the distant regions in the northeast territories of his father's kingdom.

These territories included:

1. Gaulanitis — known today as the Golan Heights.

2. Batanaea — the territory east of the Jordan River and the Sea of Galilee.

3. Trachonitis and Auranitis (or Hauran) — the southern part of modern-day Syria.

The Jews were a minority among Herod Philip's subjects. Most people under his rule were of Syrian or Arabian ancestry, but he had

Greek and Roman subjects as well, usually living in the cities. Herod Philip died in the year 34 AD after having ruled his kingdom for 37 years. Since he left no heir, the Roman Emperor Tiberius directed his territories to be added to the region of Syria.

Flavius Josephus wrote that Herod Philip was moderate and quiet in the conduct of his life and government. When Tiberius died in 37 AD, his successor, Caligula, restored the principality almost in its entirety and appointed Herod Philip's nephew, Herod Agrippa, as the new ruler — *but he's another story that we won't get into today*!

HEROD ANTIPAS

This leads us to the third son of Herod the Great — *Herod Antipas*, the same Herod before whom Jesus appeared in Luke 23:8 and who had long desired to personally meet Jesus. What do we know of this Herod?

Herod Antipas was assigned tetrarch of Galilee and Peraea (located on the east bank of the Jordan). The Roman emperor Augustus affirmed this decision, and the reign of Herod Antipas began in the year 4 BC when his father died.

The name "Antipas" is a compound of two Greek words, *anti* and *pas*. The word *anti* means *against*, and the word *pas* means *all* or *everyone*. Once compounded into one word, it means *one who is against everything and everyone*. This name alone should tell us something about the personality of this wicked ruler.

In the year 17 AD, Herod Antipas founded Tiberias, a new capitol he built to honor the Roman emperor, Tiberius. However, the construction of this city caused an enormous disturbance among his Jewish subjects when they discovered it was being built on top of an old Jewish graveyard. Because these graves had been desecrated, devout Jews refused to enter Tiberias for a very long time.

Herod Antipas tried to style himself in a way that would appeal to the Jewish people, even participating in national Jewish celebrations. But the people were not convinced by this act and viewed him as an insincere fraud. Even Jesus compared Herod Antipas to a fox — an animal that was considered to be the epitome of trickery and that was usually unclean and infected with sickness. In other words, when Jesus called Herod a fox, it was the equivalent of saying Herod was a sneaky, lying, deceiving, dishonest, infected, and sick individual. Those were pretty strong words for Jesus!

Herod Antipas' first marriage was to the daughter of an Arabian leader. However, he divorced this woman so he could marry the ex-wife of his half-brother, a woman named *Herodias*. Taking the ex-wife of one's brother was not uncommon, but Herodias was also the daughter of another half-brother, Aristobulus. In Roman law, marriage to one's niece was also permitted, but marriage to a woman who was both one's sister-in-law and one's niece was most unusual. This unusual marriage drew the attention and criticism of John the Baptist. The Gospel of Mark records that John the Baptist died because of the public stand he took against Herod Antipas' second marriage.

In the year 37, Herod Antipas' new wife, Herodias, disagreed when her brother Agrippa became king in place of Herod Philip. She thought that the royal title should not be given to Herod Agrippa but to her husband and made plans accordingly for Herod Antipas to be appointed king. Adamantly disagreeing with Herodias, the Roman emperor exiled both her and her husband to live the rest of their lives in Gaul, which is modern-day France.

Luke 23:8 tells us that Herod Antipas was eager to finally meet Jesus: "And when Herod saw Jesus, he was exceeding glad: for he was desirous to see him of a long season, because he had heard many things of him; and he hoped to have seen some miracle done by him." Notice this verse says, "And when Herod *saw* Jesus...." The word "saw" is from the Greek word *horao*, meaning *to see*; *to behold*; *to delightfully view*; *to look with scrutiny;* or *to look with the intent to examine.*

This word *horao* paints a very important picture for us of exactly what happened when Jesus finally stood before Herod Antipas. It conveys the idea that Herod was *excited* and *delighted* to finally behold the miracle-worker he had heard so much about. Once Jesus stood before him, Herod literally *looked Him over, scrutinizing and examining every detail* of the Man who appeared before him.

The next part of the verse confirms the exhilaration and jubilation Herod Antipas felt about seeing Jesus. It says, "he was *exceeding glad.*" The Greek text uses two words, *echari lian.* The word *echari* is from the word *chairo*, the Greek word for *joy*. The Greek word *lian* means *much*, *great*, or *exceedingly*. These two words together suggest *extreme excitement* or someone who is *ecstatic* about something. In other words, Herod Antipas was so "hyper" about having the chance to meet Jesus that he was nearly jumping up and down on the inside!

This should tell us how well known Jesus had become during His ministry. If Herod Antipas was this excited to meet Him, it's no wonder that the scribes and elders were apprehensive about His widespread popularity. Even the nobility longed for a chance to see Jesus' miracles!

That's why the next part of the verse says, "...for he was desirous to see him of a long season, because he had heard many things of him...." The word "desirous" is the Greek word *thelo*, which means *to will* or *to wish*. However, the construction used in this Greek phrase intensifies the *wish*, making it a *very strong wish or desire*. According to this verse, Herod had this strong desire for "a long season" — a phrase taken from the Greek words *ek hikanos chronos*. The word *hikanos* means *many, considerable*, or *much*. The word *chronos* means *time*, such as *a season, epoch, era*, or *any specified duration of time*. These words together could be translated *for many years, for a long time*, or *for many seasons*.

Why had Herod Antipas longed to see Jesus for many years? The verse says, "...because he had heard many things of him...." Jesus was a name that the Herod household had heard for years! I'm sure all three Herod boys — *Archelaus*, *Philip*, and *Antipas* — heard tales about:

1. Jesus' supernatural birth.

2. The kings from the east who had come to acknowledge Him.

3. The attempt of their father, Herod the Great, to kill Jesus by ordering all the babies in Bethlehem to be murdered.

4. Jesus and His parents slipping into Egypt and waiting for the right moment to come back into Israel.

5. The ministry of Jesus touching the nation with healing and delivering power.

Stories of Jesus must have been very familiar to the Herod household. Herod Antipas had longed for a chance to meet this famous personality for many years. Jesus was a living legend, and now He was standing in his presence!

At the end of this verse, we discover the reason that Herod Antipas was most excited to meet Jesus. The verse continues to tell us, "...he hoped to have seen some miracle done by him." The Greek word for "hoped" is *elpidzo*, meaning *to hope*. But the construction used in this verse is similar to the word *thelo*, noted above, which means *to wish*. Just as Herod's *wish* to see Jesus was *a very strong wish*, now his *hope* to see some miracle performed by Jesus was *a very strong hope* or *an earnest expectation*.

Herod was expecting to "...*have seen* some miracle done by him." The word "see" is the Greek word *horao*, the same word used in the first part of this verse when we are told that Herod was *excited to see* Jesus. Now this word is used to let us know Herod was *euphoric* about his chance to see some "miracle" done by Jesus.

The word "miracle" is the Greek word *semeion*, which is *a sign, a mark, or a token that verifies or authenticates an alleged report*. It is used in the Gospels primarily to depict *miracles and supernatural events*, which means the purpose of such miracles and supernatural events is *to verify and authenticate* the message of the Gospel.

But Luke 23:9 tells us that Jesus didn't work miracles on demand for Herod, nor did He answer the large number of questions Herod put to Him that day. As a result of Jesus' silence, the following verse tells us, "And the chief priests and scribes stood and vehemently accused him" (v. 10).

Notice that the chief priests and scribes followed Jesus from Pilate's palace to Herod's residence. When Jesus performed no miracle for Herod, the scribes and elders, most of whom belonged to the sect of the Sadducees who didn't believe in the supernatural, seized the moment to start screaming and yelling uncontrollably. The word "vehemently" is the Greek word *eutonus*, meaning *at full pitch*, *at full volume*, *strenuously*, or *vigorously*. In other words, these religious leaders weren't just slightly raising their voices; they were what we might call "screaming their heads off"! Most likely they were screaming accusations right in Jesus' face, saying things like, *"Some miracle worker You are! You have no power! You're a fraud! If You can work miracles, why don't You work one right now! You're nothing but a charlatan!"*

> **Jesus took the full brunt of this wicked ruler's wrath. Yet in the midst of all the abuse Jesus suffered, He remained quiet and held Himself calm.**

That day Herod was left with the impression that Jesus was nothing more than a spiritual fraud. Because Jesus didn't perform on demand as Herod wished, this governor's expectations were dashed, causing him to unleash his rage against Jesus.

In the short time that followed, Jesus took the full brunt of this wicked ruler's wrath. Yet in the midst of all the abuse Jesus suffered, He remained quiet and held Himself calm.

I'm sure you've been in situations when you've been railed at because you failed to meet someone's demands. Can you think of a time when something like this happened to you? How did you respond? Did you yell and scream back at that person when he vented his anger at you, or were you able to remain quiet and controlled as Jesus did that day before Herod Antipas and the chief priests and elders?

Life will occasionally take you through difficult places — such as those times when you discover that people are disappointed with your performance. If you find yourself in this kind of predicament, remember that Jesus failed to meet the expectations of Herod Antipas (although that was probably the *only* person whose expectations Jesus ever failed to meet!). When you find yourself in such a situation, go hide yourself away for a few minutes and call out to the Lord. He has been there; He understands; and He will help you know how you must respond.

Think About It

There are people in and around your life who have been longing to meet Jesus. When they encounter Him through you, will they be disappointed? Jesus told His disciples that when they saw Him, they saw the Father (John 14:7). When people see you, do they accurately see Jesus?

Herod vented his wrath when he couldn't make Jesus perform on demand. He accused Jesus of being powerless, when Jesus actually demonstrated tremendous strength by holding Himself calm and remaining silent and still. In all things, Jesus followed the Father's direction and never responded to man's attempted manipulation or threats.

In what ways would it benefit you to exercise more restraint and control over your words and responses in times of difficulty or attack?

Life brings hard places. Some you'll escape, and some you won't. At times you'll be disappointed, and other times, you'll disappoint others.

Jesus refused to meet an evil ruler's expectations and then faced the repercussions with dignity and grace. Have you developed a practice of drawing near to God, leaning deep into His arms so He can shield you in the hard places? That's a life skill you can't do without. Consider what you can do each day to cultivate that habit.

chapter

20

*A Human Ruler Mocks
the King of Kings
and Lord of Lords*

chapter

20

A Human Ruler Mocks
the King of Kings
and Lord of Lords

On that day when Jesus refused to meet Herod's expectations, Luke 23:10 tells us the chief priests and scribes were so infuriated that they stood up and "...vehemently accused him." That word "vehemently" means *at full pitch*, *at full volume*, *strenuously*, or *vigorously*. That means those men must have been screaming like crazy, out-of-control maniacs as they angrily accused Jesus of being a fraud!

Once the screaming stopped and the volume of the men's voices had lowered enough for Herod's voice to be heard, Herod gave the official order for him and his men of war to deliberately humiliate, mock, make fun of, and heckle Jesus. Suddenly the people in that room in Herod's residence turned into a booing, hissing, mocking, laughing mob, with all their venom directed toward Jesus. Luke 23:11 tells us about this event, saying, "And Herod with his men of war set him at nought, and mocked him, and arrayed him in a gorgeous robe, and sent him again to Pilate."

Notice that Herod was gathered there that day with "his men of war." Who were these men of war, and why were they at Herod's side when Jesus stood before him? The word for "men of war" in Greek is *strateuma*. This Greek word could signify *a small detachment of Roman soldiers*, but most likely it suggests that these men were Herod's personal bodyguards, selected from a larger group of soldiers because they were exceptionally trained and prepared to fight and defend if called upon — thus, the reason the *King James Version* refers to them as "men of war."

The Bible informs us that Herod, with the assistance of his body-guards, took Jesus and "set him at nought." This phrase is developed from the Greek word *exoutheneo*, a compound of the words *ek* and *outhen*. The word *ek* means *out*, and the word *outhen* is a later form of the word *ouden*, which means *nothing*. Taken together, the new word means *to make one out to be nothing*. It can be translated *to make light of, to belittle, to disdain, to disregard, to despise*, or *to treat with maliciousness and contempt*.

Jesus had already endured the insane yelling and screaming that the chief priests and elders unleashed on Him. But now Herod and his bodyguards entered center stage to start their own brand of humiliating Jesus. Luke uses the word *exoutheneo* to let us know that they were *malicious* and *vindictive* and that their behavior was *nasty* and *ugly*. Then Luke tells us that Herod and his men "mocked him." This gives us an idea of how low they sank in their ridiculing of Jesus.

The word "mocked" is the Greek word *empaidzo*, the same word used to portray the mocking behavior of the soldiers who guarded Jesus before He was taken into Caiaphas' high court (*see* Chapter 16). The word *empaidzo* meant *to play a game*. It was often used for *playing a game with children* or *to amuse a crowd by impersonating someone in a silly and exaggerated way*. It might be used in *a game of charades* when someone intends *to comically portray or even make fun of someone*.

Herod Antipas was a Roman governor — supposedly an educated, cultured, and refined man. He was surrounded by finely trained Roman soldiers who were supposed to be professional in their conduct and appearance. But these men of war, along with their ruler, descended deep into depravity as they began to put on quite a show, impersonating Jesus and the people He ministered to. They probably hammed it up, acting as if they were healing the sick; lying on the floor and quivering as if they were being liberated from devils; groping around as if they were blind and then pretending to suddenly be able to see. It was all a game of charades intended to mimic and make fun of Jesus.

Then Luke tells us, "…They arrayed him in a gorgeous robe…." The word "arrayed" is the Greek word *periballo*, which means *to throw about* or *to drape about*, as to drape around one's shoulders. The words "gorgeous robe" are the words *esthes* and *lampros*. The word *esthes* describes *a robe or garment*, while the word *lampros* depicts *something that is resplendent, glistening, or magnificent*. It was frequently used to depict *a garment made of sumptuous, brightly colored materials*.

It is doubtful that this was the garment of a soldier, for even a bodyguard of Herod would not be arrayed in such resplendent garments. In all likelihood, this was a garment worn by a politician, for when candidates were running for public office, they wore beautiful and brightly colored clothes. More specifically, however, this was almost certainly one of Herod's own sumptuous garments that he permitted to be draped around Jesus' shoulders so they could pretend to adore Him as king as part of their mockery of Him.

Although Herod apparently enjoyed this maltreatment and abuse of Jesus, Luke 23:14,15 says he could find no crime in Jesus worthy of death. Therefore, after the conclusion of these events, Herod "…sent him again to Pilate" (Luke 23:11).

When Herod sent Jesus back to Pilate, he sent Him clothed in this regal robe. One scholar notes that since this garment was one usually worn by a candidate running for office, Herod's decision to send Jesus to Pilate in this robe was the equivalent of saying, "This is no king! It's only another candidate, a pretender, who thinks he's running for some kind of office!"

When I read of what Jesus endured during the long hours before He was sent to be crucified, it simply overwhelms me. Jesus committed no sin and no crime, nor was any guile ever found in His mouth; yet He was judged more severely than the worst of criminals. Even hardened criminals would not have been put through such grueling treatment. And just think — all this happened *before* He was nailed to that wooden Cross — the lowest, most painful, debasing manner in which a criminal could be executed in the ancient world!

Jesus committed no sin and no crime, nor was any guile ever found in His mouth; yet He was judged more severely than the worst of criminals.

Before you do anything else today, why don't you take a few minutes to stop and thank Jesus for everything He went through to purchase your redemption? Salvation may have been a free gift to you, but purchasing salvation was *not* free for Jesus. It cost Him His life and His blood. This is why Paul wrote, "In whom we have redemption through his blood, the forgiveness of sins, according to the riches of his grace" (Ephesians 1:7).

And here's one more suggestion for you: Rather than keep the Good News of Jesus Christ to yourself, why don't you find an opportunity today to tell someone else all that Jesus did so he or she can be saved? God's Spirit might use you to lead someone to a saving knowledge of Jesus this very day!

Think About It

Herod Antipas actually commanded the Roman soldiers to mock Jesus, authorizing them to unleash the most vile, depraved onslaught of humiliation they could level at another human being. Jesus, the purest and the kindest in all creation, was subjected to the vilest and most perverse abuse.

Think about what Jesus went through on account of your sins. Think of what your salvation cost Him — before He even endured the pain and shame of the Cross. How long has it been since you really thanked Jesus for how much He willingly suffered for you?

Although Herod derived gruesome satisfaction from the hideous maltreatment of Jesus, he admittedly found no fault in Him.

Have you ever been subjected to treatment you did not deserve? If so, how did you respond? As you consider Jesus' example, would you respond differently to such treatment in the future?

No matter what shameful, humiliating act or attack you have experienced — either emotional or physical — Jesus can identify with it, and He can also heal its pain. People may not understand your pain, but Jesus does. He is the love of God in action, and love heals.

Think of Jesus' great love for you. Acknowledge the parts of your life where you've hidden pain and shame. Then invite Jesus' healing love to fill you up and take away the pain. He endured humiliation for you. He doesn't want you to suffer torment anymore.

chapter

21

Charged, but Not Guilty

chapter

21

Charged, but Not Guilty

When Jesus was returned to Pilate's court, Pilate assembled the chief priests and rulers. Then he told them, "…Ye have brought this man unto me, as one that perverteth the people: and, behold, I, having examined him before you, have found no fault in this man touching those things whereof ye accuse him: No, nor yet Herod: for I sent you to him; and, lo, nothing worthy of death is done unto him. I will therefore chastise him, and release him" (Luke 23:14-16).

Notice that Pilate said he had "examined" Jesus. This Greek word, *anakrinas*, means *to examine closely*, *to scrutinize*, or *to judge judicially*. Remember, Pilate was the chief legal authority of the land. He knew Roman law and was invested with power to see that Roman law was kept. From a judicial standpoint, he couldn't find a single crime Jesus had committed. Perhaps Jesus had broken some Jewish religious law, but Pilate wasn't a Jew and couldn't have cared less about Jewish law. From a purely legal standpoint, Jesus wasn't guilty. To add weight to his action, Pilate backed his view by saying, "Herod has arrived at the same conclusion as I have: This Man has committed no legal offense."

Knowing that the religious leaders were bent on seeing the shedding of Jesus' blood, Pilate offered to chastise Jesus, hoping this would appease the bloody appetite of the mob. Had this offer been accepted, the beating would have been minor. However, it would have been viewed as a warning that Jesus needed to limit His activities.

Then Pilate announced that after Jesus was chastised, he would "release" Him. When the mob heard the word "release," they jumped on the chance to reverse Pilate's decision. You see, it was a custom at this particular time of the year for one prisoner to be "released" from prison as a favor to the people. Because Israel hated the Roman occupation, many Jewish sons fought as "freedom fighters" to overthrow Roman rule. Therefore, each year when it came time for this big event, all of Jerusalem waited with anticipation to see which prisoner would be released.

By choosing to "release" Jesus at this moment, it was as if Pilate was making the choice himself which prisoner would be released — and his choice was Jesus. When the people heard of Pilate's decision, they cried out, "...Away with this man, and release unto us Barabbas: (who for a certain sedition made in the city, and for murder, was cast into prison)" (Luke 23:18,19).

Who was Barabbas? He was a notorious rabble-rouser who had been proven guilty of "sedition" in the city of Jerusalem. That word "sedition" comes from *stasis*, the old Greek word for *treason*, which refers to *the deliberate attempt to overthrow the government or to kill a head of state*.

It is interesting that treason was the very charge the Jewish leaders brought against Jesus when they accused Him of claiming to be king. However, in the case of Barabbas, the charge was *real*, for he had led a volatile insurrection against the government that resulted in a massacre. Nevertheless, Barabbas' act of bravery, although illegal and murderous, made him a hero in the minds of the local population.

Luke informs us that this Barabbas was so dangerous that they "cast" him into prison. The word "cast" is the Greek word *ballo*, meaning *to throw*, which suggests the Roman authorities wasted no time in *hurling* this low-level bandit into jail for the role he played in the bloody uprising. The Roman authorities wanted him off the streets and locked up forever!

Luke 23:20,21 says, "Pilate therefore, willing to release Jesus, spake again to them. But they cried, saying, Crucify him, crucify him." The word "willing" is the Greek word *thelo*. It would be better translated, *"Pilate therefore, wishing, longing, and desiring to release Jesus...."* Pilate searched for a way to set Jesus free, but the multitude screamed for crucifixion.

This was the first time crucifixion had been specially demanded by the crowd. Luke says the angry mob "cried" for Jesus to be crucified. The word "cried" is the word *epiphoneo*, and it means *to shout*, *to scream*, *to yell*, *to shriek*, or *to screech*. The Greek tense means they were hysterically *screaming* and *shrieking* at the top of their voices — totally out of control and without pause.

Pilate appealed to them again: "...Why, what evil hath he done? I have found no cause of death in him: I will therefore chastise him, and let him go" (Luke 23:22). Again the Roman governor hoped that a beating might satisfy the people's bloody hunger, but "...they were instant with loud voices, requiring that he might be crucified. And the voices of them and of the chief priests prevailed" (v. 23).

The words "they were instant" is the Greek word *epikeima*, a compound of the words *epi* and *keimai*. The word *epi* means *upon*, and the word *keimai* means *to lay something down*. When compounded together, this word meant that the people began *to pile evidence on top* of Pilate, nearly *burying him* in reasons why Jesus had to be crucified. To finish this quarrel, they threatened him, saying, "...If thou let this man go, thou art not Caesar's friend: whosoever maketh himself a king speaketh against Caesar" (John 19:12).

Pilate was taken aback by the threat of treason these Jewish leaders were bringing against him. Once he heard these words, he knew they had him in a trap — and there was only one way legally for him to get out of the mess he was in. He had to make a choice: He could either set Jesus free and sacrifice his own political career, or he could deliver Jesus to be crucified and thus save himself.

When confronted with these two stark choices, Pilate decided to sacrifice Jesus and save himself. But as he turned Jesus over to the masses, Pilate first wanted to make it clear to everyone who was listening that he didn't agree with what they were doing. This is why Matthew 27:24 tells us, "When Pilate saw that he could prevail nothing, but that rather a tumult was made, he took water, and washed his hands before the multitude, saying, I am innocent of the blood of this just person: see ye to it."

Pilate had to make a choice: He could either set Jesus free and sacrifice his own political career, or he could deliver Jesus to be crucified and thus save himself.

Pay careful attention to the fact that Pilate "...took water, and washed his hands...." Water, of course, is symbolic of a cleansing agent, and hands are symbolic of our lives. For instance, with our hands we touch people, we work, and we make money. In fact, nearly everything we do in life, we do with our hands. This is why Paul told us to "lift up holy hands" when we pray and worship (1 Timothy 2:8). When we lift our hands to God, it is the same as lifting our entire lives before Him, because our hands represent our lives.

In Bible times, the washing of hands was a ritual often used symbolically for the removal of one's guilt. So when Pilate washed his hands in that basin of water and publicly declared, "I am clear of all guilt regarding the blood of this just person!" he was demonstrating what he believed to be his total innocence in this matter.

As long as Pontius Pilate thought he could stand with Jesus and keep his own position as well, he protected Jesus. But the moment Pilate realized that saving Jesus would mean he would have to sacrifice his own position in life, he quickly changed his tune and gave in to the demands of the mob of people who were screaming all around him.

Can you think of times in your own life when your walk with Jesus put you in an unpopular position with your peers? What did you do when you realized your commitment to the Lord was going to jeopardize your job or your status with your friends? Did you sacrifice your friendship and your status, or did you sacrifice your commitment to the Lord?

Let's decide today to never make the mistake of sacrificing our relationship with Jesus for other people or other things. Instead, let's resolve to stand by Jesus, regardless of the situation or the personal cost we may have to pay for staying faithful to Him.

Remember what Jesus said: "Whoever finds his life will lose it, and whoever loses his life for my sake will find it" (Matthew 10:39 *NIV*). When you hang on to the wrong things, your wrong choices always cost you the most. On the other hand, when you let go of things you count dear and choose to give everything you have to Jesus, you always receive back far more than you could ever ask or imagine.

Think About It

When faced with the choice of enforcing the truth but sacrificing his career, Pilate caved into a lie by sacrificing Jesus to the will of an angry mob. Integrity comes with a price, but the consequences of abandoning integrity for self-preservation are even costlier.

Can you think of some ways in which you've chosen self-preservation above being faithful to Jesus?

Pilate made an outward show of washing his hands to demonstrate what he considered to be his own innocence. He did it in an attempt to distance himself from the bloodthirsty crowd and to prove that he didn't really support the decision he felt trapped into making. Yet Pilate's willing compromise with the crowd locked him within their ranks.

What choices are you faced with on a daily basis that could lure you into compromise? How do you respond to those opportunities? Do you see a need to respond differently?

What do you suppose is the underlying emotion or belief that would prompt a person to go along with public opinion, even when that opinion is contrary to what he or she really believes? Do you know how you'd respond if you were ever thrust into such a situation? Think about it.

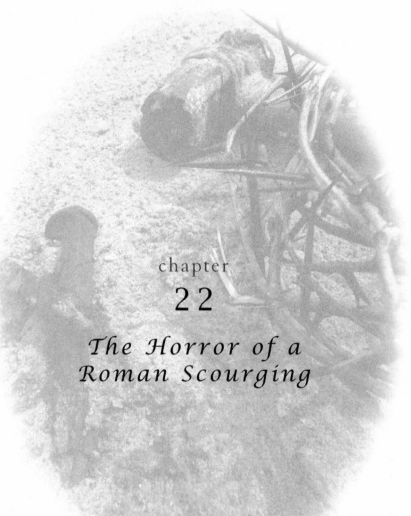

chapter

22

The Horror of a
Roman Scourging

chapter

22

The Horror of a
Roman Scourging

What was it like for a prisoner to be scourged in New Testament times? From what materials was a scourge made? How did it feel when the straps of a scourge whipped across a person's back and body? What effects did a scourging have on the human body?

Matthew 27:26 tells us that Pilate "had scourged Jesus" before he delivered Him to be crucified, so we need to understand what it meant to be "scourged." The word "scourged" is the Greek word *phragello*. It was one of the most horrific words used in the ancient world because of the terrible images that immediately came to mind when a person heard it. Let me tell you a little about the process of scourging and what it did to the human body. I believe this explanation is important so you can understand more completely what Jesus endured *before* He was taken to be crucified.

When a decision was made to scourge an individual, the victim was first stripped *completely* naked so his entire flesh would be open and uncovered to the beating action of the torturer's whip. Then the victim was bound to a two-foot-high scourging post. His hands were tied over his head to a metal ring, and his wrists were securely shackled to that ring to restrain his body from movement. When in this locked position, the victim couldn't wiggle or move, trying to dodge the lashes that were being laid across his back.[6]

Romans were professionals at scourging. They took special delight in the fact that they were the "best" at punishing a victim with this brutal act. Once the victim was harnessed to the post and stretched over it, the Roman soldier began to put him through unimaginable torture. One writer notes that the mere anticipation of the whipping caused the victim's body to grow rigid, the muscles to knot in his stomach, the color to drain from his cheeks, and his lips to draw tight against his teeth as he waited for the first sadistic blow that would begin tearing his body open.

The scourge itself consisted of a short, wooden handle with several 18- to 24-inch-long straps of leather protruding from it. The ends of these pieces of leather were equipped with sharp pieces of metal, wire, glass, and jagged fragments of bone. This was considered to be one of the most feared and deadly weapons of the Roman world. It was so ghastly that the mere threat of scourging could calm a crowd or bend the will of the strongest rebel. Even the most hardened criminal recoiled from the prospect of being submitted to the vicious beating of a Roman scourge.

Most often, two torturers were utilized to carry out this punishment, simultaneously lashing the victim from both sides. As these dual whips struck the victim, the leather straps with their sharp, jagged objects descended and extended over his entire back. Each piece of metal, wire, bone, or glass cut deeply through the victim's skin and into his flesh, shredding his muscles and sinews.

Every time the whip pounded across the victim, those straps of leather curled tortuously around his torso, biting painfully and deeply into the skin of his abdomen and upper chest. As each stroke lacerated the sufferer, he tried to thrash about but was unable to move because his wrists were held so firmly to the metal ring above his head. Helpless to escape the whip, he would scream for mercy that this anguish might come to an end.

Every time the torturers struck a victim, the straps of leather attached to the wooden handle would cause multiple lashes as the sharp objects at the end of each strap sank into the flesh and then raked across the victim's body. Then the torturer would jerk back, pulling hard in order to tear whole pieces of human flesh from the body. The victim's back, buttocks, back of the legs, stomach, upper chest, and face would soon be disfigured by the slashing blows of the whip.

Historical records describe a victim's back as being so mutilated after a Roman scourging that his spine would actually be exposed. Others recorded how the bowels of a victim would actually spill out through the open wounds created by the whip. The Early Church historian Eusebius wrote: "The veins were laid bare, and the very muscles, sinews, and bowels of the victim were open to exposure."[7]

The Roman torturer would so aggressively strike his victim that he wouldn't even take the time to untangle the bloody, flesh-filled straps as he lashed the whip across the victim's mangled body over and over again. If the scourging wasn't stopped, the slicing of the whip would eventually flay the victim's flesh off his body.

With so many blood vessels sliced open by the whip, the victim would begin to experience a profuse loss of blood and bodily fluids. The heart would pump harder and harder, struggling to get blood to the parts of the body that were bleeding profusely. But it was like pumping water through an open water hydrant; there was nothing to stop the blood from pouring through the victim's open wounds.

This loss of blood caused the victim's blood pressure to drop drastically. Because of the massive loss of bodily fluids, he would experience excruciating thirst, often fainting from the pain and eventually going into shock. Frequently the victim's heartbeat would become so irregular that he would go into cardiac arrest.

This was a Roman scourging.

According to Jewish law in Deuteronomy 25:3, the Jews were permitted to give 40 lashes to a victim, but because the fortieth lash usually proved fatal, the number of lashes given was reduced to 39, as Paul noted in Second Corinthians 11:24. But the Romans had no limit to the number of lashes they could give a victim, and the scourging Jesus experienced was at the hands of Romans, not Jews. Therefore, it is entirely possible that after the torturer pulled out his whip to beat Jesus, he may have laid more than 40 lashes across Jesus' body. In fact, this is even probable in light of the explosive outrage the Jews felt for Jesus and the terrible mocking He had already suffered at the hands of Roman soldiers.

So when the Bible tells us that Jesus was scourged, we now know exactly what type of beating Jesus received that night. What toll did the cruel Roman whip exact on Jesus' body? The New Testament doesn't tell us exactly what Jesus looked like after He was scourged, but Isaiah 52:14 says, "As many were astonied at thee; his visage was so marred more than any man, and his form more than the sons of men."

If we take this scripture literally for what it says, we can conclude that Jesus' physical body was marred nearly beyond recognition. As appalling as this sounds, it was only the overture to what was to follow. Matthew 27:26 continues to tell us, "...and when he had scourged Jesus, *he delivered him to be crucified.*" This scourging was only the preparation for Jesus' crucifixion!

Every time I think about the scourging Jesus received that day, I think of the promise God makes to us in Isaiah 53:5. This verse says, "But he was wounded for our transgressions, he was bruised for our iniquities: the chastisement of our peace was upon him; and with his stripes we are healed." In this verse, God declares that the price for our healing would be paid by those stripes that were laid across Jesus' back.

In First Peter 2:24, the apostle Peter quoted Isaiah 53:5. He told his readers, "...By whose stripes ye were healed." The word "stripes" used in this verse is *molopsi*, which describes *a full-body bruise.* It refers to *a terrible lashing that draws blood and that produces discoloration and swelling of the entire body.* When Peter wrote this verse, he wasn't speaking by revelation but by memory, for he vividly remembered what happened to

Jesus that night and what His physical appearance looked like after His scourging.

After graphically reminding us of the beating, bleeding, and bruising that Jesus endured, Peter jubilantly declared that it was by these same stripes that we are "healed." The word "healed" is the Greek word *iaomai* — a word that clearly refers to *physical healing*, as it is a word borrowed from the medical term to describe *the physical healing or curing of the human body*.

For those who think this promise refers to spiritual healing only, the Greek word emphatically speaks of *the healing of a physical condition*. This is a real promise of bodily healing that belongs to all who have been washed in the blood of Jesus Christ!

Jesus' broken body was the payment God demanded to guarantee our physical healing! Just as Jesus willfully took our sins and died on the Cross in our place, He also willfully took our sicknesses and pains on Himself when they tied Him to the scourging post and laid those lashes across His body. That horrific scourging paid for our healing!

> *Just as Jesus willfully took our sins and died on the Cross in our place, He also willfully took our sicknesses and pains on Himself when they tied Him to the scourging post and laid those lashes across His body.*

If you need healing in your body, you have every right to go to God and ask for healing to come flooding into your system. It's time for you to dig in your heels and hold fast to the promise of God's Word, releasing your faith for the healing that belongs to you.

Jesus went through this agony for *you*, so don't let the devil tell you that it's God's will for you to be sick or weakly. Considering the pain Jesus endured to bear your sicknesses that day, isn't that enough evidence to convince you how much He wants you to be physically well?

Think About It

The vicious, sadistic scourging Jesus experienced mutilated and disfigured His body beyond recognition. The awful price for our healing was paid by the scourging Jesus received.

Are you currently dealing with some form of sickness, infirmity, or disease in your body? Meditate on how Jesus' body was scourged so your body could be healed. Consider how valuable you and your body must be to God that He would allow His Son to pay such a price.

The Roman whip ripped and gouged Jesus' body until His blood gushed forth like water through an open hydrant and spilled upon the ground.

That blood was Jesus' very life being poured out for *you*. Think about the kind of love that would compel Jesus to pour out His life's blood so you could have mercy instead of judgment and your debt could be paid in full.

Jesus' broken body was the payment required to pay for our physical healing.

Do you need healing? Think about the horrific scourging Jesus willfully endured so you could have every right to go before God and confidently expect to obtain your healing. Then honor the gift of Jesus' life by gratefully receiving His healing provision for your physical body.

chapter

23

Tortured for You

chapter

23

Tortured for You

After Jesus was scourged, Pilate delivered Him to the Roman soldiers so they could initiate the crucifixion process. However, first these soldiers dragged Jesus through the worst mockery and humiliation of all. Matthew 27:27-29 describes what Jesus went through at this stage of His ordeal: "Then the soldiers of the governor took Jesus into the common hall, and gathered unto him the whole band of soldiers. And they stripped him, and put on him a scarlet robe. And when they had platted a crown of thorns, they put it upon his head, and a reed in his right hand: and they bowed the knee before him, and mocked him, saying, Hail, King of the Jews!"

Verse 27 says the soldiers "...took Jesus into the common hall, and gathered unto him the whole band of soldiers." The "common hall" was the open courtyard in Pilate's palace. Since Pilate rotated between several official royal residences in Jerusalem, this could have been his palace at the Tower of Antonia (*see* Chapter 5). It also could have been his residence at the magnificent palace of Herod, located on the highest part of Mount Zion. All we know for sure is that the courtyard was so large, it was able to hold "the whole band of soldiers." This phrase comes from the Greek word *spira*, referring to *a cohort* or *a group of 300 to 600 Roman soldiers*.

Hundreds of soldiers filled the courtyard of Pilate's residence to participate in the events that followed. Matthew 27:28 says, "And they stripped him, and put on him a scarlet robe." First, the soldiers "stripped him." The word "stripped" is the Greek word *ekduo*, which means *to totally unclothe* or *to fully undress*. Nakedness was viewed as a disgrace, a shame, and an embarrassment in the Jewish world. Public nakedness was associated with pagans — with their worship, their idols, and their statues.

As children of God, the Israelites honored the human body, made in the image of God. Thus, to publicly parade someone's naked body was a great offense. We can know, then, that when Jesus was stripped naked in front of 300 to 600 soldiers, it went against the grain of His entire moral view regarding what was right and wrong.

Once Jesus stood naked before them, the soldiers then "…put on him a scarlet robe." The Greek phrase is *chlamuda kokkinen*, from the word *chlamus* and *kokkinos*. The word *chlamus* is the Greek word for *a robe* or *a cloak*. It could refer to a soldier's cloak, but the next word makes it more probable that this was one of Pilate's old cloaks. You see, the word "scarlet" is the Greek word *kokkinos*, a word that describes *a robe that has been dyed a deep crimson or scarlet color*, which is suggestive of *the deeply colored crimson and scarlet robes worn by royalty or nobility*. Did this cohort of Roman soldiers who worked at Pilate's residence pull an old royal robe from Pilate's closet and bring it to the courtyard for the party? It seems that this is the case.

As Matthew continues the account, we find out what happened next: After the soldiers "…had *platted* a crown of thorns, they put it upon his head…." The word "platted" is the Greek word *empleko*. Thorns grew everywhere, including in the imperial grounds of Pilate. These thorns were long and sharp like nails. The soldiers took vines that were loaded with sharp and dangerous thorns; then they carefully wove together those razor-sharp, prickly, jagged vines until they formed a tightly woven, dangerous circle that resembled the shape of a crown.

Afterward, the soldiers "…put it upon his head…." Matthew uses the Greek word *epitithimi*, a word that implies they *violently pushed* or *forcefully shoved* this crown of thorns onto Jesus' head. These thorns would have been extremely painful and caused blood to flow profusely from His brow. Because the thorns were so jagged, they would have created terrible wounds as they scraped across Jesus' scalp and literally tore the flesh from His skull.

Matthew called it a "crown" of thorns. The word "crown" is from the Greek word *stephanos*, the word that described a coveted *victor's crown*. These soldiers intended to use this mock crown to make fun of Jesus. Little did they know that Jesus was preparing to win the greatest victory in history!

After forcing the crown of thorns down onto Jesus' brow, the soldiers put "...a *reed* in his right hand...." There were many beautiful ponds and fountains in Pilate's inner courtyard where long, tall, hard "reeds" grew. While Jesus sat there before them clothed in a royal robe and crown of thorns, one of the soldiers must have decided that the picture was not quite complete and pulled a "reed" from one of the ponds or fountains to put in Jesus' hand.

This reed represented the ruler's staff, as seen in the famous statue called "Ave Caesar," which depicted Caesar holding a staff or scepter in his hand. The same image, also showing a scepter in the right hand of the emperor, appeared on coins that were minted in the emperor's honor and in wide circulation.

Once the soldiers had draped a discarded royal robe about Jesus' shoulders, set a crown of thorns so deeply into His head that blood drenched His face, and stuck a reed from Pilate's ponds or fountains in Jesus' right hand, they then "...bowed the knee before him, and mocked him, saying, Hail, King of the Jews!" (Matthew 27:29). The word "bowed" is the Greek word *gonupeteo*, meaning *to fall down upon one's knees*. One by one, the cohort of soldiers passed before Jesus, dramatically and comically dropping to their knees in front of Him as they laughed at and mocked Him.

The word "mocked" is the Greek word *empaidzo*, the same word used to describe the mocking of Herod and his bodyguards (*see* Chapter 20). As

Pilate's soldiers mocked Jesus, they said to Him, "Hail, King of the Jews!" The word "hail" was an acknowledgment of honor used when saluting Caesar. Thus, the soldiers shouted out this mock salute to Jesus as they would to a king to whom honor was due.

Matthew 27:30 goes on to tell us, "And they spit upon him, and took the reed, and smote him on the head." The word "they" refers to the entire cohort of soldiers who were present in Pilate's courtyard that night.

So as each soldier passed by Jesus, he would first mockingly bow before Him; then he'd lean forward to spit right in Jesus' blood-drenched face. Next the soldier would grab the reed from Jesus' hand and strike Him hard on His already wounded head. Finally, he would stick the reed back in Jesus' hand to make Him ready for the next soldier to repeat the whole process.

The Greek clearly means that *the soldiers repeatedly struck Jesus again and again on the head*. Here was another beating that Jesus endured, but this time it was with the slapping action of a hard reed. This must have been excruciatingly painful for Jesus, since His body was already lacerated from the scourging and His head was deeply gashed by the cruel crown of thorns.

When all 300 to 600 soldiers were finished spitting and striking Jesus with the reed, Matthew 27:31 tells us that "…they took the robe off from him, and put his own raiment on him, and led him away to crucify him." The robe wrapped around Jesus had no doubt meshed into His wounds, for it took a great amount of time for so many soldiers to parade before Him. Therefore, it must have been terrifically painful for Jesus when they jerked this robe off His back and the material ripped free from the dried blood that had coagulated on His open lacerations.

But this would be the last act of torture Jesus would endure in this stage of His ordeal. After putting His own clothes back on Him, the soldiers led Him from the palace to the place of execution.

As the soldiers mocked Jesus that day, hailing Him as king in derision and ridicule, they were unaware that they were actually bowing their knees to the One before whom they would one day stand and give an account for their actions. When that day comes, bowing before Jesus will be no laughing matter, for *everyone* — including those very soldiers who mocked Jesus — will confess that Jesus is Lord!

As the soldiers mocked Jesus that day, hailing Him as king in derision and ridicule, they were unaware that they were actually bowing their knees to the One before whom they would one day stand and give an account for their actions.

Yes, a day is soon coming when the human race will bow their knees to acknowledge and declare that Jesus is the King of kings. Philippians 2:10,11 talks about that day: "That at the name of Jesus every knee should bow, of things in heaven, and things in earth, and things under the earth; and that every tongue should confess that Jesus Christ is Lord, to the glory of God the Father."

If you have a friend who doesn't know Jesus yet, don't you think it's time for you to introduce him to Jesus Christ? Your friend will one day bow before Him anyway. The question is, from which place will he bow before Jesus — from Heaven, from earth, or from hell?

Everyone in Heaven will bow low before Jesus on that day, as will everyone who is alive on earth at His coming and all who have gone to hell because they didn't bow before Him while they lived on this earth. So the big question is not *if* a person will bow before Him, but *from which place* he or she will choose to do so.

Isn't it your responsibility to help lead your friends and acquaintances to Jesus? God's Spirit will empower you to speak the Gospel to them. If you pray before you speak to them, the Holy Spirit will prepare their hearts to hear the message.

I encourage you to stop long enough today to quiet your heart and ask the Lord to help you speak the truth to those friends, acquaintances, and fellow workers whom you interact with every day. Their eternal destiny may very well depend on it.

Think About It

The Roman soldiers took brutality to an entirely different level. They derived sick pleasure from inflicting not only physical pain, but also mental anguish and emotional distress. By stripping Jesus naked, the soldiers mocked His moral piety. By dressing Him in royal-like garb, they ridiculed His nobility.

Think about the compassion and empathy Jesus feels for you when you are mocked, ridiculed, and deliberately humiliated. Trust Him. He will save you.

The crown of thorns, the robe, and the pond-reed staff each depicted a ruler's symbols of authority. One day every eye will behold Jesus crowned with a royal diadem and robed in the splendor of the glory that is His alone. On that day, every knee will bow, of saints and scoffers alike.

What are you doing to prepare others to meet Jesus on that day? What are you doing to prepare yourself?

Jesus suffered unfathomable agony from the vicious beatings by religious leaders and the horrific scourging and violent mocking by Roman soldiers. All this transpired *before* He was led away to endure the

most painful, traumatic, and debasing execution known at the time —
crucifixion.

Since God didn't spare Jesus from paying such a high price for your
sin, consider how willing He is to provide for your every need through
Jesus.

chapter

24

Golgotha:
The Place of the Skull

24

Golgotha:
The Place of the Skull

When the soldiers brought Jesus out from the residence of Pilate, Jesus was already carrying the crossbeam that would serve as the upper portion of His Cross.

Most Roman crosses were shaped like a "T." The upright post had a notched groove at the top into which the crossbeam was placed after a victim had been tied or nailed to it. The crossbeam, normally weighing about 100 pounds, was carried on the back of the victim to the place of execution.

According to Roman law, once a criminal was convicted, he was to carry his own cross to the place of execution if his crucifixion was to occur somewhere other than the place of the trial. The purpose for exposing criminals heading for crucifixion to passersby was to remind those who watched of Roman military power. At the place of execution, vultures flew overhead, waiting to swoop down and start devouring the dying carcasses left hanging on the crosses. In the nearby wilderness, wild dogs anxiously waited for the newest dead bodies, dumped by the executioners, to become their next meal.

After a person was declared guilty, a crossbeam would be laid across his back and a herald would walk ahead of him, proclaiming his crime. A sign with the person's crime written on it would also be made, later to be hung on the cross above his head. Sometimes the sign bearing the person's crime would be hung from his neck, so all the spectators who lined the streets to watch him walk by would know what crime he committed. This was the very type of sign that was publicly displayed on the Cross above Jesus' head, with the crime He was charged with — "King of the Jews" — written in Hebrew, Greek, and Latin.

Carrying such a heavy weight for a long distance would be difficult for any man, but especially for one who had been as severely beaten as Jesus. The heavy crossbeam on which He was destined to be nailed pressed into His torn back as He carried it to the place of execution. Although the Bible does not state the reason why, we may assume that the Roman soldiers forced Simon of Cyrene to help because Jesus was so drained and exhausted from the abuse He had suffered.

Little is known of Simon of Cyrene, except that he was from Cyrene, the capital of the province of Libya that was situated approximately 11 miles south of the Mediterranean Sea. Matthew 27:32 informs us that the Roman soldiers "compelled him to bear his cross." The word "compelled" is the Greek word *aggareuo*. It means *to compel*; *to coerce*; *to constrain*; *to make*; or *to force someone into some kind of compulsory service*.

Matthew 27:33 says, "And when they were come unto a place called Golgotha, that is to say, a place of a skull." This scripture has been the center of controversy for several hundred years, for many have attempted to use this verse to geographically identify the exact location of Jesus' crucifixion. Some denominations allege that the place of Jesus' crucifixion was inside modern-day Jerusalem, while others assert that the name Golgotha refers to a site outside the city that from a distance looks like a skull. However, the earliest writings of the Church fathers say this phrase "a place of a skull" refers to something very different.

An early Christian leader named Origen, who lived from 185-253 AD, recorded that Jesus was crucified on the spot where Adam was buried and where his skull had been found. Whether or not this is true, there *was* an early Christian belief that Jesus had been crucified near Adam's burial place. As this early story goes, when the earthquake occurred as Jesus hung on the Cross (Matthew 27:51), His blood ran down the Cross into a crack in the rock below and fell on the skull of Adam. This belief is so entrenched in early Christian tradition that Jerome, one of the most prominent scholars of the Early Church, referred to it in a letter in 386 AD.[8]

Interestingly, Jewish tradition states that Noah's son, Shem, buried Adam's skull near the city of Jerusalem. Tradition also says this burial place was guarded by Melchizedek, who was the priest-king of Salem (Jerusalem) during the time of Abraham (*see* Genesis 14:18). Unknown to most Western believers, this history is so accepted that it is considered a major theme of Orthodox doctrine, and the skull of Adam appears consistently at the base of the Cross in both paintings and icons. If you ever see a skull at the base of a crucifix, you can know that it symbolizes Adam's skull that was allegedly found buried at the site of Jesus' crucifixion.

These extremely interesting traditions, although unprovable, have retained strong support throughout 2,000 years of Christian history. If it were true, it would be quite amazing that the Second Adam, Jesus Christ, died for the sins of the world exactly on the spot where the first Adam, the original sinner, was buried. If Jesus' blood ran down the crack in the stone and fell upon Adam's skull, as tradition says, it would be very symbolic of Jesus' blood covering the sins of the human race that originated with Adam.

But what can we definitely know about the place of Jesus' crucifixion?

We definitely know that Jesus was crucified like a criminal by the Roman government just outside the walls of the ancient city of Jerusalem. Whether or not He was crucified at the place of Adam's skull is interesting but not important. What is vital for us to know and understand is that Jesus died for the sins of the entire human race — and that includes you and me!

Today we may not be able to say with certainty exactly where Jesus was crucified, but in our hearts and minds, we should meditate on the scriptures that speak of His crucifixion. Sometimes life moves so fast that we tend to forget the enormous price that was paid for our redemption. Salvation may have been given to us as a free gift, but it was purchased with the precious blood of Jesus Christ. *Thank God for the Cross!*

Sometimes life moves so fast that we tend to forget the enormous price that was paid for our redemption.

This question of where Jesus was crucified is a good example of the way people tend to get distracted by unimportant issues and, as a result, miss the main point God wants to get across to them. People have argued and debated for centuries about the accurate location of the crucifixion, when the truth they should have been focusing on is that Jesus was crucified for their salvation! The apostle Paul wrote, "...Christ died for our sins according to the scriptures; and that he was buried, and that he rose again on the third day according to the scriptures" (1 Corinthians 15:3,4). Of this, we can be sure!

Aren't you thankful that Jesus' blood purchased the forgiveness for all of mankind's sin? It is true that through Adam's disobedience, sin entered the world and death was passed on to all men. But just as sin entered the world through Adam, the gift of God came into the world through the obedience of Jesus Christ. Now the grace of God and the free gift of righteousness abound to all who have called upon Jesus Christ to be the Lord of their lives (*see* Romans 5:12-21). Now every believer has the glorious privilege of reigning in life as a joint heir with Jesus Himself!

Think About It

It is interesting to note that Orthodox tradition has held for 2,000 years that Golgotha is the burial place of Adam's skull. Whether or not that is true is not the point. The point is this: The blood of Jesus cleansed all sin that originated with Adam.

God always goes to the root of a matter. To what root issues in your own life do you need to apply the cleansing blood of Jesus Christ?

Notice the only "crime" Jesus was convicted of: being the King of the Jews. Are you living your life in such a way — publicly and privately — that the only thing people can accuse and convict you of is fulfilling your divine purpose?

Simon of Cyrene was forced to help Jesus carry His actual Cross. Jesus has invited you to pick up *your* cross — your own opportunity for obedience to the plan of God — and to follow Him daily.

What opportunity for obedience is before you today that will require you to die to your own will and preferences? In what way will you follow Jesus in that situation?

chapter
2 5
Crucified!

25

Crucified!

When Jesus arrived at Golgotha, the Bible says, "They gave him vinegar to drink mingled with gall..." (Matthew 27:34). According to Jewish law, if a man was about to be executed, he could request a narcotic, mingled together with wine, which would help alleviate the pain of his execution. The word "gall" in this verse refers to this special painkiller.

There was a group of kind women in Jerusalem who made it their good deed to help anesthetize the pain of people who were dying horrific deaths. These women wanted to eliminate as much pain and misery as possible for the scores of people being crucified by the Romans. Therefore, they produced the homemade painkiller that Matthew tells us about in this verse.

Jesus was offered this anesthetic twice — once before His crucifixion and once while He was dying on the Cross (*see* Matthew 27:34,48). In both instances, Jesus turned down the offer and refused to drink it, for He knew He was to fully consume the cup the Father had given Him to drink.

Verse 35 begins, "And they crucified him...." The word "crucified" is the Greek word *staurao*, from the word *stauros*, which describes *an upright, pointed stake that was used for the punishment of criminals*. This word was used to describe those who were *hung up, impaled, or beheaded and then publicly displayed*. It was always used in connection with *public execution*. The point of hanging a criminal publicly was to bring further humiliation and additional punishment to the accused.

Crucifixion was indisputably one of the cruelest and most barbaric forms of punishment in the ancient world. Flavius Josephus described crucifixion as "the most wretched of deaths." It was viewed with such horror that in one of Seneca's letters to Lucilius, Seneca wrote that suicide was preferable to crucifixion.

Different parts of the world had different kinds of crucifixion. For example, in the East the victim was beheaded and then hung on public display. Among the Jews, the victim was first stoned to death and then hung on a tree. Deuteronomy 21:22,23 commanded, "And if a man have committed a sin worthy of death, and he be to be put to death, and thou hang him on a tree: his body shall not remain all night upon the tree, but thou shalt in any wise bury him that day; (for he that is hanged is accursed of God;)...."

But at the time Jesus was crucified, the grueling act of crucifixion was entirely in the hands of the Roman authorities. This punishment was reserved for the most serious offenders, usually for those who had committed some kind of treason or who had participated in or sponsored state terrorism.

Because Israel hated the occupying Roman troops, insurrections frequently arose among the populace. As a deterrent to stop people from participating in revolts, crucifixion was regularly practiced in Jerusalem. By publicly crucifying those who attempted to overthrow the government, the Romans sent a strong signal of fear to those who might be tempted to follow in their steps.

Once the offender reached the place where the crucifixion was to occur, he was laid on the crossbeam he carried (*see* Chapter 24) with his arms outstretched. Then a soldier would drive a five-inch (12.5-centimeter) iron nail through each of his wrists — not the palms of his hands — into the crossbeam. After being nailed to the crossbeam, the victim was hoisted up by rope, and the crossbeam was dropped into a notch on top of the upright post.

When the crossbeam dropped into the groove, the victim suffered excruciating pain as his hands and wrists were wrenched by the sudden jerking motion. Then the weight of the victim's body caused his arms to be pulled out of their arm sockets. Josephus writes that the Roman soldiers "out of rage and hatred amused themselves by nailing their prisoners in different postures."[9] Crucifixion was truly a vicious ordeal.

Once the victim's wrists were secured in place on the crossbeam, the feet came next. First, the victim's legs would be positioned so that the feet were pointed downward with the soles pressed against the post on which the victim was suspended. A long nail would then be driven between the bones of the feet, lodged firmly enough between those bones to prevent it from tearing through the feet as the victim arched upward, gasping for breath.

In order for the victim to breathe, he had to push himself up by his feet, which were nailed to the vertical beam. However, because the pressure on his feet became unbearable, it wasn't possible for him to remain long in this position, so eventually he would collapse back into the hanging position.

As the victim pushed up and collapsed back down again and again over a long period of time, his shoulders eventually dislocated and popped out of joint. Soon the out-of-joint shoulders were followed by the elbows and wrists. These various dislocations caused the arms to be extended up to nine inches longer than usual, resulting in terrible cramps in the victim's arm muscles and making it impossible for him to push himself upward any longer to breathe. When he was finally too exhausted and could no longer push himself upward on the nail lodged in his feet, the process of asphyxiation began.

Jesus experienced all of this torture. When He dropped down with the full weight of His body on the nails that were driven through His wrists, it sent horrific, excruciating pain up His arms to register in His brain. Added to this torture was the agony caused by the constant grating of Jesus' recently scourged back against the upright post every time He pushed up to breathe and then collapsed back to a hanging position.

Due to extreme loss of blood and hyperventilation, the victim would begin to experience severe dehydration. We can see this process in Jesus' own crucifixion when He cried out, "...I thirst" (John 19:28). After several hours of this torment, the victim's heart would begin to fail. Next his lungs would collapse, and excess fluids would begin filling the lining of his heart and lungs, adding to the slow process of asphyxiation.

When the Roman soldier came to determine whether or not Jesus was alive or dead, he thrust his spear into Jesus' side. One expert pointed out that if Jesus had been alive when the soldier did this, the soldier would have heard a loud sucking sound caused by air being inhaled past the freshly made wound in the chest. But the Bible tells us that water and blood mixed together came pouring forth from the wound the spear had made — evidence that Jesus' heart and lungs had shut down and were filled with fluid. This was enough to assure the soldier that Jesus was already dead.

It was customary for Roman soldiers to break the lower leg bones of a person being crucified, making it impossible for the victim to push himself upward to breathe and thus causing him to asphyxiate at a much quicker rate. However, because of the blood and water that gushed from Jesus' side, He was already considered dead. Since there was no reason for the soldiers to hasten Jesus' death, His legs were never broken.

This, my friend, is a brief taste of Roman crucifixion.

The above description of crucifixion was exactly what Jesus experienced on the Cross when He died for you and me. This is why Paul wrote, "And being found in fashion as a man, he humbled himself, and became obedient unto death, even the death of the cross" (Philippians 2:8). In Greek the emphasis is on the word "even," from the Greek word *de*, which dramatizes the point that Jesus lowered Himself to such an extent that He died *even* the death of a Cross — the lowest, most humiliating, debasing, shameful, painful method of death in the ancient world.

Now you understand why the kind women of Jerusalem prepared homemade painkillers for those being crucified. The agony associated with crucifixion is the reason they offered Jesus this "gall," once before the crucifixion began and again as He hung on the Cross.

Meanwhile, the soldiers near the foot of the Cross "...parted his garments, casting lots..." (Matthew 27:35). They didn't understand the great price of redemption that was being paid at that moment as Jesus hung asphyxiating to death, His lungs filling with fluids so that He couldn't breathe.

According to Roman custom, the soldiers who carried out the crucifixion had a right to the victim's clothes. Jewish law required that the person being crucified would be stripped naked. So there Jesus hung, completely open and naked before the world, while His crucifiers literally distributed His clothes among themselves!

Making this distribution of clothes even cheaper was the fact that the soldiers "cast lots" for His garments. The Gospel of John records that "...when they had crucified Jesus, took his garments, and made four parts, to every soldier a part; and also his coat: now the coat was without seam, woven from the top throughout. They said therefore among themselves, Let us not rend it, but cast lots for it..." (John 19:23,24).

This account informs us that four soldiers were present at Jesus' crucifixion. The four parts of His clothing that were distributed among them were His head gear, sandals, girdle, and the *tallith* — the outer garment that had fringes on the bottom. His "coat," which was "without seam," was a handmade garment that was sewn together from top to bottom. Because it was specially handmade, this coat was a very expensive piece of clothing. This was the reason the soldiers chose to cast lots for it rather than tear it into four parts and spoil it.

When the Bible refers to "casting lots," it indicates a game during which the soldiers wrote their names on pieces of parchment, wood, or stones and then dropped all four pieces with their names written on them into some kind of container. Because the Roman soldiers who helped crucify Jesus were remotely located, it is probable that one of them pulled off his helmet and held it out to the other soldiers. After the others dropped their names in the helmet, the soldier shook it to mix up the four written names and then randomly withdrew the name of the winner.

It is simply remarkable that all of this was taking place as Jesus was pushing down on that huge nail lodged in His feet so He could gasp for breath before sagging back down into a hanging position. As Jesus' strength continued to drain away and the full consequence of man's sin was being realized in Him, the soldiers at the foot of the Cross played a game to see who would get His finest piece of clothing!

Matthew 27:36 says, "And sitting down they watched him there." The Greek word for "watch" is the word *tereo*, which means *to guard*. The Greek tense means *to consistently guard* or *to consistently be on the watch*. It was the responsibility of these soldiers to keep things in order, to keep watch over the crucifixion site, and to make sure no one came to rescue Jesus from the Cross. So as they cast lots and played games, the soldiers were also keeping watch out of the corners of their eyes to make certain no one touched Jesus as He hung dying on the Cross.

When I read about the crucifixion of Jesus, it makes me want to repent for the callousness with which the world looks upon the Cross today. In our society, the cross has become a fashion item, decorated with gems, rhinestones, gold, and silver. Beautiful crosses of jewelry adorn women's ears and dangle at the bottom of gold chains and necklaces. The symbol of the cross is even tattooed on people's flesh!

The reason this is so disturbing to me is that in beautifying the Cross to make it pleasing to look upon, people have forgotten that it wasn't beautiful or lavishly decorated at all. In fact, the Cross of Jesus Christ was *shocking* and *appalling*.

Jesus' totally naked body was flaunted in humiliation before a watching world. His flesh was ripped to shreds; His body was bruised from head to toe; He had to heave His body upward for every breath He breathed; and His nervous system sent constant signals of excruciating pain to His brain. Blood drenched Jesus' face and streamed from His hands, His feet, and from the countless cuts and gaping wounds the scourging had left upon His body. In reality, the Cross of Jesus Christ was a disgusting, repulsive, nauseating, stomach-turning sight — so entirely different from the attractive crosses people wear today as jewelry or as a part of their attire.

Whether it's the Easter season or any other season of the year, it would be good for all of us as believers to take a little time to remember what the Cross of Jesus Christ was really like. If we don't deliberately choose to meditate on what He went through, we will never fully appreciate the price He paid for us. How tragic it would be if we lost sight of the pain and the price of redemption!

When we fail to remember what it cost Jesus to save us, we tend to treat our salvation cheaply and with disregard.

When we fail to remember what it cost Jesus to save us, we tend to treat our salvation cheaply and with disregard. That's why the apostle Peter wrote, "Forasmuch as ye know that ye were not redeemed with corruptible things, as silver and gold, from your vain conversation received by tradition from your fathers; but with the precious blood of Christ, as of a lamb without blemish and without spot" (1 Peter 1:18,19).

The kind women of Jerusalem wanted to anesthetize Jesus to remove His pain. But He refused their painkiller and entered into the experience of the Cross with all His faculties.

Let's not allow the world to anesthetize *us*, causing us to overlook, forget, or esteem lightly the enormous price our Savior paid for each of us on the Cross of Calvary.

Think About It

The cross symbolizes one of the most barbaric forms of execution in history. When we beautify it, we tend to minimize the shocking and appalling reality of all it represents.

Take the time to reflect deliberately upon the tortuous death Jesus willingly died for you. Think about the excruciating pain and the comprehensive price that was required for your redemption. Jesus gave you His all. Can you give Him any less?

The horror and humiliation of death on the Cross defies comprehension. Yet Jesus refused to be drugged or dulled to the agony of it. Instead, He drank the dregs of the cup He initially besought the Father to remove in Gethsemane.

Think deeply about the hideous process of Jesus' death and the callous indifference of the soldiers who cast lots for His clothing as He died naked before the world. As Jesus died, He forgave. He forgave those who played a part in His death. He forgave your sin, which was the very reason for His death. If Jesus could go through that degree of suffering because of your sins against the Father and then forgive you, how can you justify refusing to release in forgiveness those who have sinned against you?

First John 3:16 (*NKJV*) states, "By this we know love, because He laid down His life for us. And we also ought to lay down *our* lives for the brethren...." What are some ways you can lay down your life for others?

chapter
26
It Is Finished!

chapter

2 6

It Is Finished!

When Jesus therefore had received the vinegar,
he said, It is finished:
and he bowed his head, and gave up the ghost.

— John 19:30

The Cross of Jesus Christ is the most precious emblem to those of us who call Jesus the Lord of our lives. We love the Cross and cherish it because of the price that was paid 2,000 years ago when Jesus died for our sins. The Cross represents our forgiveness, our freedom, our redemption. We love it so much that we adorn our churches and homes with crosses, and women even wear them around their necks. But when the pure Lamb of God hung on that Cross we deem so precious — naked, beaten, and bleeding profusely before a watching world — it was a ghastly sight. Indeed, it was the most horrendous moment in human history.

No death was more scandalous than death on a cross. Such a death was dreadful and hideous, designed to discredit and tarnish the memory of the one dying. Blood drenched Jesus' torso, pouring from His head and brow, running like rivers from the deeply torn flesh in His hands and feet. The effect of the scourging that Jesus had received in Pilate's palace began to take its toll as His body swelled up and became horribly discolored. His eyes were matted with the blood that poured from the wounds in His brow — wounds caused by the crown of thorns that bore down into His skull as the soldiers pushed it hard upon His head. The whole scene was ugly, unsightly, repulsive, sickening, vile, foul, and revolting.

In the Jewish world, nakedness was a particularly profound shame. Because the body was made in the image of God, the Jewish people believed it was a great dishonor to display a naked body. So as if Jesus' suffering had not already been enough, He experienced the ultimate act of degradation and shame as He hung on the Cross, naked and exposed before all those who watched the unfolding drama.

Approximately 700 years earlier, the prophet Isaiah correctly prophesied Jesus' appearance on the Cross. In Isaiah 52:14, the prophet wrote with a sense of horror, "As many were astonied at thee; his visage was so marred more than any man, and his form more than the sons of men." In Isaiah 53:2, Isaiah continued, "...He hath no form nor comeliness; and when we shall see him, there is no beauty that we should desire him."

Jesus had been put through horrendous forms of torture and had been atrociously abused and battered. As a result, "...His face and His whole appearance were marred more than any man's and His form beyond that of the sons of men..." (Isaiah 52:14 *AMP*). In the *New International Version*, this verse is translated to say, "...His appearance was so disfigured beyond that of any human being and his form marred beyond human likeness...."

In Isaiah 53:3-5, Isaiah continued to vividly describe Jesus' sacrifice. He wrote, "He is despised and rejected of men; a man of sorrows, and acquainted with grief: and we hid as it were our faces from him; he was despised, and we esteemed him not. Surely he hath borne our griefs, and carried our sorrows: yet we did esteem him stricken, smitten of God, and afflicted. But he was wounded for our transgressions, he was bruised for our iniquities: the chastisement of our peace was upon him; and with his stripes we are healed."

When Jesus died on that Cross:

- He bore our griefs.

- He carried our sorrows.

- He was wounded for our transgressions.

- He was bruised for our iniquities.

- He was chastised for our peace.

- He was scourged for our healing.

As Jesus approached death, the Bible tells us, "They gave him vinegar to drink mingled with gall...." (Matthew 27:34). As we saw in Chapter 25, a man who was to be executed could request a narcotic, mingled together with wine, which would help alleviate the pain of his execution. As noted before, the word "gall" in this verse is a special Greek word that refers to a painkiller that was mingled together with wine. John 19:30 tells us that "When Jesus therefore had received the vinegar, he said, It is finished: and he bowed his head, and gave up the ghost."

"It is finished" is a translation of the Greek word *tetelestai*, the perfect indicative passive tense of the word *telos*, which means *to end*; *to bring to completion*; *to bring to a conclusion*; *to complete*; *to accomplish*; *to fulfill*; or *to finish*. One scholar notes that anything that has reached *telos* has arrived at completion, maturity, or perfection. There were many nuances to this word, but four or them have great significance with this defining moment of Christ's sacrifice.

First, this was Jesus' exclamation that He had finished the work the Father had sent Him to do. The work having been fully completed, Jesus bowed His head and died. One writer has noted that when a servant was sent on a mission and then later returned to his master, he would say, *"Telelestai"* — meaning, *"I have done exactly what you requested"* or *"The mission is now accomplished."*

In that moment when Jesus cried out, He was exclaiming to the entire universe that He had faithfully fulfilled the Father's will and that the mission was now accomplished. No wonder Jesus shouted — for this was the greatest victory in the history of the human race! He had been faithful to His assignment even in the face of unfathomable challenges.

But now the fight was over, and Jesus could cry out to the Father, *"I have done exactly what You asked Me to do!"* or *"The mission is accomplished!"*

Second, the word *tetelestai* was the equivalent of the Hebrew word spoken by the high priest when he presented a sacrificial lamb without spot or blemish. Annually the high priest entered the Holy of Holies, where he poured the blood of that sacrificial spotless lamb on the mercy seat of the Ark of the Covenant. The moment that blood touched the mercy seat, atonement was made for the people's sins for one more year — when once again, the high priest would enter beyond the veil of that sacred room to offer blood. This was done year after year to obtain the annual, temporary forgiveness of sin.

Jesus had been faithful to His assignment even in the face of unfathomable challenges. But now the fight was over, and Jesus could cry out to the Father, "I have done exactly what You asked Me to do!"

But when Jesus hung on the Cross, He was both Lamb and High Priest. In that holy moment as our Great High Priest, Jesus offered His own blood for the permanent removal of sin. He offered up the perfect sacrifice of which every Mosaic sacrifice was a type and symbol — and in that instant, there remained no more need of offering for sin.

Jesus entered into the Holy Place and offered His own blood — a sacrifice so complete that God never again required the blood of lambs for forgiveness. As Hebrews 9:12 says, "Neither by the blood of goats and calves, but by his own blood he entered in once into the holy place, having obtained eternal redemption for us."

Thus, when Jesus said, "It is finished!" He was declaring the end of sacrifice, because the ultimate Sacrifice had finally been made! Atonement was *completed*, *perfected*, and *fully accomplished*. It was done once and for all — *finished forever*!

Third, in a secular sense, the word *tetelestai* was used in the business world to signify *the full payment of a debt*. When a debt had been fully paid off, the parchment on which the debt was recorded was stamped with *tetelestai*, which meant the debt had been *paid in full*. This means that once a person calls Jesus the Lord of His life and personally accepts His sacrifice, no debt of sin exists for that person any longer. The debt is wiped out because Jesus paid the price for sin that no sinner could *ever* pay.

Jesus took our place. He paid the debt of sin we owed. And when we by faith repent and receive Him as Lord, *we are set free*! This is why Paul wrote, "In whom we have redemption through his blood, even the forgiveness of sins" (Colossians 1:14).

When Jesus uttered those words, "It is finished!" it was His declaration that the debt was *fully satisfied*, *fulfilled*, and *complete*. His blood utterly and completely cleansed us forever. It was *far-reaching* and *all-embracing* for all of us who put our faith in Him.

Fourth, in classical Greek times, the word *tetelestai* depicted *a turning point when one period ended and another new period began*. When Jesus exclaimed, "It is finished!" it was indeed a turning point in the entire history of mankind, for at that moment the Old Testament came to an end — finished and closed — and the New Testament began. The Cross was "the Great Divide" in human history. When Jesus cried out, "It is finished!" He was shouting that the Old Covenant had ended and the New Covenant had begun!

In that divine moment when Jesus cried, "It is finished," all the Old Testament prophecies about Jesus' earthly ministry were fulfilled. The justice of God had been fully met and satisfied by the Lamb of God. At that moment, the sacrifices of the Old Testament permanently ceased, for the perfect Sacrifice had laid down His life for the salvation of mankind. Jesus' mission was accomplished. Thus, He could cry out that His task was complete!

Never forget that because Jesus was willing to offer His own blood for the full payment of our sinful debt, we are forgiven and utterly debt-free. "PAID IN FULL" has been stamped on our past sinful record because Jesus paid the price for our redemption with His own blood.

Isaiah said, "Surely he hath borne our griefs, and carried our sorrows: yet we did esteem him stricken, smitten of God, and afflicted. But he was wounded for our transgressions, he was bruised for our iniquities: the chastisement of our peace was upon him; and with his stripes we are healed" (Isaiah 53:4,5). So remember:

❖ If you are consumed with grief, remember that Jesus bore *your* grief.

❖ If you are overwhelmed with sorrows, remember that He carried *your* sorrow.

❖ If you are trapped in a life of transgression, remember that He was wounded for *your* transgressions.

❖ If you are living in sin, you can be forgiven because He was bruised for *your* iniquities.

❖ If you are tormented and have no peace, remember that He was chastised for *your* peace.

❖ If you are physically or mentally sick, remember that He was wounded for *your* healing.

Jesus paid the price for your salvation, for your liberation, for your physical healing, and for your complete restoration. When the price for your forgiveness was complete, Jesus bowed His head and died. God's justice had been fulfilled. The Old Covenant had ended, and the New Covenant had begun. It was the fulfillment of one and the beginning of another.

Think of the price Jesus paid and what His death accomplished for you. Doesn't it make you want to stop for a few minutes to thank Him for what He has done for you? Where would you be today if Jesus had not died on the Cross for you? Why don't you take a little time right now to express your heartfelt thanksgiving to Jesus for paying the debt you never could have paid!

Think About It

Jesus endured excruciating painful torture, humiliation, and shame on Calvary's Cross. Death by crucifixion was considered so scandalous that it forever marked how the one who died in that manner was remembered.

Meditate on the kind of death Jesus died in order to purchase your freedom from the power of sin. If sin requires that kind of penalty, why would you allow it to linger in any area of your life?

As the ground was splattered with Jesus' sinless, holy blood, the entire universe witnessed His faithful fulfillment of the Father's will. Jesus won the greatest victory in the history of the human race — a victory we were incapable of winning for ourselves.

Consider how much it cost Jesus to proclaim, "It is finished." Ask yourself: *Choice by choice, day by day, am I willing to pick up MY cross — my opportunity to obey the will of the Father for my life?*

If every debt and credit-card bill you owed was suddenly paid off, how would you act? Jesus paid in full your debt to sin. Consider the far-reaching implication of that truth. Sickness, torment, grief, and guilt have no right to oppress you or demand anything from you. Jesus paid your bill, cancelled your debt, and left you with a zero balance! How should that truth influence what you say and do on a daily basis?

chapter
27

*The Day
the Earth Trembled*

27

The Day
the Earth Trembled

The historians Phlegon, Thaddus, and Julius Africanus all referred to the darkness that covered the earth at the time of Jesus' crucifixion. Critics of the Bible have attempted to explain away this supernatural darkness by alleging that it was due to an eclipse of the sun. This is impossible, however, for the Passover occurred at the time of a full moon.[10]

The Bible informs us that the darkening of the sky started at the sixth hour (*see* Matthew 27:45; Mark 15:33; Luke 23:45). This is significant, for the sixth hour (noontime) was the very moment that the high priest Caiaphas, arrayed in his full priestly garments, began the procession in which he would enter the temple courts to slaughter a pure, spotless Passover lamb.

In fact, a great number of unblemished lambs were slaughtered in the temple courts during those hours of darkness — one lamb slaughtered for every household in Israel (unless, of course, the household was too small). This supernatural darkness that covered the land lasted until the ninth hour — about the time when the sacrifices of the Passover lambs would be coming to an end.

It was at this moment that Jesus cried out, *"It is finished!"* (John 19:30). As He heaved upward to breathe for the last time, Jesus gathered enough air to speak forth a victory shout. His assignment was complete! After proclaiming those words with His last ounce of strength, Matthew 27:50 tells us that He "…yielded up the ghost."

What Matthew tells us next is simply *amazing*! He writes, "And, behold, the veil of the temple was rent in twain from the top to the bottom…." The word "behold" is the Greek word *idou*. This is a very difficult word to translate, for it carries such intense feeling and emotion. The *King James Version* most often translates this word as *behold*. But in our contemporary world, it might be better rendered, *Wow!*

This word *idou* carries the idea of *shock*, *amazement*, and *wonder*. It's almost as if Matthew says, *"Wow! Can you believe it? The veil of the temple itself rent in twain from top to bottom!"* Matthew wrote about this event many years after the fact, yet he was still so dumbfounded by what happened that day that he exclaimed in effect, *"Wow! Look what happened next!"*

There were two veils inside the temple — one at the entrance to the Holy Place and a second at the entrance to the Holy of Holies. Only the high priest was allowed to pass through the second veil once a year during the Festival of Atonement. That second veil was 60 feet high, 30 feet wide, and an entire handbreadth in thickness! One early Jewish writing states that the veil was so heavy, it took 300 priests to move or manipulate it. Humanly speaking, it would have been impossible to tear such a veil.

At the exact moment Jesus was breathing His last breath on the Cross at Golgotha, Caiaphas the high priest was standing at his station in the inner court of the temple, finishing the sacrifices of the spotless Passover lambs. In the same instant that Jesus exclaimed, "It is finished!" — miles away from Golgotha inside the temple at Jerusalem — an inexplicable, mystifying supernatural event occurred. The massive, fortified veil that stood before the Holy of Holies was suddenly split in half from the top all the way to the bottom!

The sound of that veil splitting must have been deafening as it ripped and tore, starting from the top and going all the way down to the floor. It was as if invisible, divine hands had reached out to grab it, rip it to shreds, and discard it.

Imagine how shocked Caiaphas must have been when he heard the ripping sounds inside the temple and then watched as the veil was torn in half, leaving the two sides of the once-massive curtain lying collapsed to his right and his left. Just think what must have gone through this evil high priest's mind when he saw that the way to the Holy of Holies was opened — and that God's Presence was no longer there!

You see, when Jesus was lifted up on the Cross, that Cross became the eternal mercy seat on which the blood of the final Sacrifice was sprinkled. Once that Sacrifice was made, it was no longer necessary for a high priest to continually make sacrifices year after year, for Jesus' blood had now settled the issue forever!

For this cause, God Himself ripped the veil of the temple in half, declaring that the way to the Holy of Holies was now available to everyone who came to Him through the blood of Jesus! This is why the apostle Paul wrote that Jesus "...hath broken down the middle wall of partition between us" (Ephesians 2:14).

Jesus' death was such a dramatic event that even the earth reacted to it. Matthew 27:51 says, "...The earth did quake, and the rocks rent." The word "earth" is the word *ges*, which describes *the whole earth*. The word "quake" is the Greek word *seiso*, which means *to shake*, *to agitate*, or *to create a commotion*. It is where we get the word for a *seismograph*, the apparatus that registers the intensity of an earthquake. It is interesting to note that Origen, the early Christian leader, recorded that there were "great earthquakes" at the time of Jesus' crucifixion.[11]

I find it so amazing that although Israel rejected Jesus and the Roman authorities crucified Him, creation *always* recognized Him! During His life on this earth, the waves obeyed Him; water turned to wine at His command; fishes and bread multiplied at His touch; the atoms in water solidified so He could walk across it; and the wind ceased when He spoke to it. So it should come as no surprise that Jesus' death was a traumatic event for creation. The earth shook, trembled, and shuddered at the death of its Creator, for it instantly felt its loss.

The earth shuddered so violently when Jesus died that even "...the rocks rent...." The word "rocks" is *petra*, referring to *large rocks*. The other word that could have been used for "rocks" is the word *lithos*, which meant *small stones*. But Matthew tells us that *huge, large rocks* were "rent" by the shaking of the earth. The word "rent" is *schidzo*, meaning *to rend, to tear, to violently tear asunder*, or *to terribly fracture*. This was a *serious* earthquake! It makes me realize all over again the incredible significance of the death of Jesus Christ!

> *The earth shook, trembled, and shuddered at the death of its Creator, for it instantly felt its loss.*

When Jesus' blood was accepted at the Cross as final payment for man's sin, the need to habitually offer sacrifices year after year was eliminated. The Holy of Holies, a place limited only to the high priest once a year, has now become open and accessible to all of us! As "believer-priests," each of us can now enjoy the presence of God every day. This is why Hebrews 10:19,22 says, "Having therefore, brethren, boldness to enter into the holiest by the blood of Jesus.... Let us draw near with a true heart in full assurance of faith, having our hearts sprinkled from an evil conscience...."

The way into the Holy of Holies has been thrown wide open to us. Now it's up to us to take a few minutes each day to enter into the presence of God to worship Him and to make our requests known. Jesus died for us so we could "...come boldly unto the throne of grace, that we may obtain mercy, and find grace to help in time of need" (Hebrews 4:16). He has done His part. Now it's up to us to come with boldness before the throne of grace to receive the divine help God has already provided for us.

Think About It

God Himself ripped the veil of the Holy of Holies in half from top to bottom. In so doing, He declared that man could now come freely to stand in His holy presence. Furthermore, God demonstrated that sin no longer separated Him from man. Once He had walked with man in the Garden before Adam sinned. Now that the penalty for sin was paid through Jesus, God would once more walk freely among those who chose to walk with Him.

How can you take full advantage of your opportunity to experience ongoing fellowship with the Father? What do you need to do differently?

The earth and its elements have always recognized and responded to the voice and the presence of the One who created them.

How readily do *you* respond to the voice and the presence of the Holy Spirit who resides within you?

God personally removed all barriers that blocked man from His holy presence.

Are you tolerating any unnecessary hindrances in your life that prevent you from coming boldly before the throne of God?

chapter

28

A Burial of Love

chapter

28

A Burial of Love

When it was time for Jesus' body to be brought down from the Cross, Pilate received a surprise visit from a high-ranking member of the Sanhedrin who was a secret follower of Jesus. His name was Joseph, from the city of Arimathea; thus, we know this man as *Joseph of Arimathea*. Another high-ranking member of the Sanhedrin accompanied Joseph — also a secret disciple of Jesus. This second man's relationship with Jesus began with a secret visit in the middle of the night, recorded in John 3:1-21. The second admirer's name was *Nicodemus*.

Let's begin with Joseph of Arimathaea and see what we know of him. To obtain an accurate picture of this man, we must turn to Mark 15:42 and 43, which says, "And now when the even was come, because it was the preparation, that is, the day before the sabbath, Joseph of Arimathaea, an honourable counseller, which also waited for the kingdom of God, came, and went in boldly unto Pilate, and craved the body of Jesus."

This verse tells us that Joseph of Arimathea was an "honorable counselor." The Greek word for "honorable" is *euschemon*, a compound of the words *eu*, meaning *well* or *good*, and the word *schema*, meaning *form*, often referring to *an outward appearance*. When compounded together, the new word means *a good outward appearance*. It refers to *people who have a good reputation*; *people who have a good standing in society*; or *people who are prominent, influential, and wealthy*. The word "counselor" is the Greek word *bouleutes*, the word for *a member of the Sanhedrin*. This is the same word used to describe *Roman senators*. By using this word *bouleutes*, Mark tells us that Joseph of Arimathea's position in the land of Israel was one of great honor and respect.

The above verse also tells us that he "waited for the kingdom of God." The Greek word for "waited" is *prosdechomai*. Other examples of this word are found in Acts 24:15, where it describes *a hope* or *an expectation*. In Romans 16:2, Paul uses this word to tell the Roman church *to receive* Phebe, suggesting that they *fully receive* and *embrace* her. In Hebrews 10:34, it is translated *to take*, and it means *to fully and completely take something without reservation of hesitation*. So when Mark 15:43 tells us that Joseph of Arimathea "...waited for the kingdom of God...," this doesn't refer to a do-nothing, "hang-around-and-see-what-happens" kind of waiting. Joseph was earnestly looking for and anticipating the Kingdom. He was inwardly ready *to take it*, *to fully receive it*, and *to embrace it without any reservation or hesitation*.

This explains why Joseph was attracted to the ministry of Jesus. Because of Joseph's deep hunger and longing to see the Kingdom of God, he ventured out to see this Jesus of Nazareth. *Spiritual hunger is always a prerequisite to receiving the Kingdom of God*, and Joseph of Arimathea possessed that hunger. His willingness to think "outside the circle" of how others in the Sanhedrin thought no doubt made him unique in the supreme council. However, it appears that the other members of the council shut their eyes and tolerated Joseph due to his prominent position and extreme wealth.

Next, Mark tells us that Joseph of Arimathea went "boldly unto Pilate." Although he was undoubtedly known for his spiritual hunger, John 19:38 informs us that this Joseph had never publicly announced that he was a follower of Jesus "for fear of the Jews."

As a member of the Sanhedrin, Joseph was well aware of the exultation the supreme council members felt over Jesus' death. If it became known that Joseph was the one who took the body and buried it, it could place him in considerable jeopardy. Therefore, going to Pilate to request that he might remove the body of Jesus before the Sabbath began was an act of bravery on Joseph's part.

Joseph's desire to take the body of Jesus and prepare it for burial was so powerful that Mark 15:43 says he "craved the body of Jesus." The word "craved" is the Greek word *aiteo*, a word that means *to be adamant in requesting and demanding something*. In the New Testament, the word *aiteo* is used to portray *a person addressing a superior*, as in this case when Joseph of Arimathea appealed to Pilate. The person may *insist* or *demand* that a need be met, but he approaches and speaks to his superior with *respect*. Therefore, although Joseph showed respect toward Pilate's position, he also presented a strong demand to the governor, adamantly insisting that Jesus' body be released to him.

The word "body" is the Greek word *ptoma*, which always referred to *a dead body* and is often translated as the word "corpse." The Roman custom was to leave the body hanging on the cross until it rotted or until the vultures had picked away at it. Afterward, they discarded of the corpse in the wilderness, where it was eaten by wild dogs. The Jews, however, held the human body in great honor because it was made in the image of God. Even those who were executed by the Jews were respected in the way they were handled after death. Thus, it was not permitted for a Jew's body to hang on a cross after sunset or to be left to rot or for the birds to devour.

Mark 15:44,45 says, "And Pilate marvelled if he were already dead: and calling unto him the centurion, he asked him whether he had been any while dead. And when he knew it of the centurion, he gave the body to Joseph."

At this point, *Nicodemus* enters the picture. The third chapter of John gives the greatest insight into Nicodemus. It says, "There was a man of the Pharisees, named Nicodemus, a ruler of the Jews: the same came to Jesus by night, and said unto him, Rabbi, we know that thou art a teacher come from God: for no man can do these miracles that thou doest, except God be with him" (John 3:1,2).

John 3:1 tells us that Nicodemus was a "Pharisee." The word "Pharisee" means *the separated ones*. This means they viewed themselves separated by God for His purposes. Thus, they were extremely committed and even fanatical in their service to God.

During the time Jesus lived, the Pharisees were the most respected and esteemed religious leaders in Israel. The Pharisees believed in the supernatural and earnestly waited for the arrival of the Messiah, contrary to the Sadducees who did *not* believe in the supernatural and did *not* wait for the Messiah's coming. The Pharisees held strictly to the Law, whereas the Sadducees took a more liberal approach to the Law that the Pharisees found unacceptable. Flavius Josephus, the famous Jewish historian, was a Pharisee, as was Gamaliel (*see* Acts 5:34) and the apostle Paul before he was converted to Christ on the road to Damascus (*see* Philippians 3:5).

Verse 1 goes on to tell us that Nicodemus was "a ruler of the Jews." The word "ruler" is the Greek word *archon*, which means *the chief one*, *ruler*, or *prince*. This word was used to denote *the rulers of local synagogues and members of the Sanhedrin* who were the *highest authorities* in the land. Due to this high-ranking position, Nicodemus, like Joseph of Arimathea, was *prominent*, *influential*, and *wealthy*.

Nicodemus' notoriety among the Jews in Jerusalem was the reason he visited Jesus by night. His fame most likely created a stir every time he passed through the city. Therefore, Nicodemus wanted to avoid visiting Jesus by day, as it would draw attention to the fact that he was spending time with a teacher the Sanhedrin viewed to be a maverick and out of their control. Consequently, he came to Jesus by night when his visit would not be observable.

What he told Jesus during this visit reveals much about the spiritual hunger that Nicodemus possessed. First, he called Jesus "Rabbi." The word itself means *great*, but it was used as a title of respect only in reference to the great teachers of the Law. The Pharisees loved to be called "Rabbi," for they viewed themselves as the chief keepers of the Law.

For Nicodemus to call Jesus "Rabbi" was remarkable indeed. The Jewish leader would never have used that title unless he had already heard Jesus interpret the Law and thereby judged His ability to do so. The fact that Nicodemus called Jesus by this privileged title, given only to those who were viewed as the greatest theologians in Israel, tells us that he was very impressed with Jesus' knowledge of the Scriptures.

This means that Nicodemus, like Joseph of Arimathea, was open-minded enough to receive from people who were "outside the circle" of what most religious people viewed as acceptable. In fact, Nicodemus was so hungry to find a touch of God that it appears he himself visited Jesus' meetings that had just been conducted in the city of Jerusalem.

John 2:23 says, "Now when he [Jesus] was in Jerusalem at the passover, in the feast day, many believed in his name, when they saw the miracles which he did." When Nicodemus visited with Jesus, he referred to these miracles, saying in John 3:2, "...Rabbi, we know that thou art a teacher come from God: for no man can do these miracles that thou doest, except God be with him."

It seems that Nicodemus had come close enough to these miracle meetings to personally view the miracles. This must have been the occasion when he heard Jesus teach and deemed Him worthy of the title "Rabbi." As a Pharisee, Nicodemus believed in the supernatural. He was so moved by the miracles and so convinced of their legitimacy that he wanted to personally meet Jesus and ask Him questions. In the conversation that followed, Jesus told Nicodemus, "...Verily, verily, I say unto thee, Except a man be born again, he cannot see the kingdom of God" (John 3:3). The famous conversation that followed has been read, quoted, and preached all over the world for 2,000 years.

After Joseph of Arimathea received permission to remove Jesus' body from the Cross, he took the body to begin preparations for burial. John 19:39 tells us what happened next: "And there came also Nicodemus, which at the first came to Jesus by night, and brought a mixture of myrrh and aloes, about an hundred pound weight."

This verse tells us Nicodemus "…brought a mixture of myrrh and aloes, about an hundred pound weight…." "Myrrh" was an expensive yellowish-brown, sweet-smelling gum resin that was obtained from a tree and had a bitter taste. It was chiefly used as a chemical for embalming the dead. "Aloes" was a sweet-smelling fragrance derived from the juice pressed from the leaves of a tree found in the Middle East. It was used to ceremonially cleanse, to purify, and to counteract the terrible smell of the corpse as it decomposed. Like myrrh, this substance was also very expensive and rare — yet the Bible tells us that Nicodemus "brought a mixture" of both substances — about a hundred pounds' worth!

Nicodemus' cost for this offering of love must have been out of sight! Only a rich man could have purchased such a massive combination of these costly, uncommon substances. Nicodemus obviously intended to fully cover the body of Jesus, so he spared no cost in preparing the body for burial, demonstrating his love for Jesus right up to the very end.

John goes on to tell us, "Then took they the body of Jesus, and wound it in linen clothes with the spices, as the manner of the Jews is to bury" (v. 40). The word for "linen" is the Greek word *othonion*, which describes *a cloth made of very fine and extremely expensive materials* that was fabricated primarily in Egypt. Nobles in that day were known to pay very high prices to have robes made for their wives from this material.

When Lazarus came forth from the tomb after being resurrected by Jesus, he was "…bound hand and foot with graveclothes: and his face was bound about with a napkin…" (John 11:44). This shows that Lazarus was bound with bandages made of strips of material. However, the word *othonion* tends to suggest that Jesus was carefully laid in a large linen sheet of fine weave. Specially prepared spices were then mingled between the folds of this high-priced garment in which Jesus' dead body was wrapped.

This is an amazing story of two men who dearly loved Jesus. Although Joseph and Nicodemus lived in circumstances that made it difficult for them to publicly follow Jesus, they chose to follow Him to their fullest capability. When Jesus died, they continued to demonstrate their deep love for Him, treating His dead body with tender care and using their personal wealth to bury Him with honor. As far as they understood at the time, this was their last opportunity to show Jesus how much they loved Him, and they were going to take full advantage of it!

Jesus taught, "For where your treasure is, there will your heart be also" (Matthew 6:21). When these two men used their wealth to bury Jesus, they illustrated that their hearts were with Jesus. He was their highest priority, so they invested their assets in showing their love for Him. They literally sowed their money into the ground when they bathed Jesus in 100 pounds of those rare substances, wrapped Him in an expensive cloth, and then buried Him in a rich man's tomb.

When these two men used their wealth to bury Jesus, they illustrated that their hearts were with Jesus. He was their highest priority, so they invested their assets in showing their love for Him.

If people were to look at the way you spend your finances, would they be able to see that Jesus is the highest priority in your life? Do you treat Him with honor and respect in the way you serve Him, or is He the last priority on your list? According to the words of Jesus, what you do with your finances really does tell the truth about what you love the most. So what would He say about your financial choices? What does the way you spend money reveal about how much you love Jesus?

As Joseph of Arimathea and Nicodemus honored Jesus in death, we are called to honor Jesus with everything we possess as we serve Him every day of our lives. We are privileged to serve Jesus, so let's make the choice to upgrade our giving and our living in every realm so that all glory goes to Him!

Think About It

Joseph of Arimathea displayed great love for Jesus as he boldly and insistently requested that Pilate hand over to him the body of Jesus. Joseph risked his reputation and acceptance among the Jews when he identified himself as a follower of Jesus. Joseph also invested great wealth into Jesus' burial with 100 pounds of burial spices, an expensive, imported burial shroud, and Joseph's own exquisitely carved tomb.

Has your identification with Jesus ever cost you anything of value? What would observers come to understand about your commitment to Him by the way you choose to spend or invest your finances?

What conscious daily choices do you make to serve and honor God with your life?

Spiritual hunger, much like natural hunger, compels a person to take action. Those who hunger and thirst for God, for His approval, and for His ways will be satisfied.

How would you define your current level of spiritual hunger? Has your appetite for the things of God decreased or increased over the past year?

chapter

29

Buried and Sealed

29

Buried and Sealed

John's Gospel tells us that near the crucifixion site was a garden. The Greek word for "garden" is *kepos*, and it refers *to any garden with trees and spices*. It can also be translated as *an orchard*. The same word is used in John 18:1 to describe *the Garden of Gethsemane*, which was *an olive tree orchard*.

All four Gospels suggest that this tomb was near the place where Jesus was crucified, but John 19:42 says, "…The sepulchre was nigh at hand." The word "nigh" is the Greek word *aggus*, meaning *nearby*. Most crucifixions were performed along a roadside. Evidently this garden was located in an orchard-like place, just down the road from where Jesus was crucified.

John 19:41 tells us that in the garden was "…a new sepulchre, wherein was never man yet laid." The word "new" is the Greek word *kainos*, meaning *fresh* or *unused*. This doesn't necessarily mean that the tomb had recently been made but that it was a tomb that had never been used — thus, the reason John writes, "…wherein was never man yet laid."

Matthew, Mark, and Luke all record that this tomb belonged to Joseph of Arimathea, suggesting that it was the tomb he had prepared for his own burial. The fact that it was a tomb "hewn out in the rock" (Matthew 27:60; Mark 15:46; Luke 23:53) confirms the personal wealth of Joseph of Arimathea. Only royalty or wealthy individuals could afford to have their tombs carved out of a wall of stone or in the side of a mountain. Poorer men were buried in simple graves.

The word "hewn" in Matthew, Mark, and Luke comes from the Greek word *laxeuo*, meaning not only *to cut out*, but *to polish*. It implies that it was *a special tomb*, *a highly developed tomb*, *a refined tomb*, or *a tomb that was splendid and expensive*. Isaiah 53:9 had prophesied that the Messiah would be buried in a rich man's tomb, and the word *laxeuo* strongly suggests that this was indeed the expensive tomb of a very rich man.

John 19:42 says, "There laid they Jesus...." The word "laid" comes from the word *tithimi*, which means *to set*, *to lay*, *to place*, *to deposit*, or *to set in place*. As used here, it portrays the careful and thoughtful placing of Jesus' body in its resting place inside the tomb. Luke 23:55 tells us that after Jesus' body was placed in the tomb, the women who came with Him from Galilee "...beheld the sepulchre, and how his body was laid." The word "beheld" in Greek is *theaomai*, from which we get the word *theater*. The word *theaomai* means *to gaze upon*, *to fully see*, or *to look at intently*. This is very important, for it proves the women *inspected* the tomb, *gazing upon* the dead body of Jesus *to see* that it had been honorably laid in place.

Mark 15:47 identifies these women as Mary Magdalene and Mary the mother of Joses and says that these women "...beheld where he was laid" at the tomb. The imperfect tense is used in Mark's account, alerting us to the fact that these women took their time in making sure Jesus was properly laid there. It could be translated, "*They carefully contemplated where he was laid.*" If Jesus had still been alive, those who buried Him would have known it, for they spent substantial time preparing His body for burial. Then after His dead body was deposited into the tomb, they lingered there, checking once again to see that the body was treated with the greatest love and attention.

Once they were certain everything was done correctly, Joseph of Arimathea "...rolled a great stone to the door of the sepulchre, and departed" (Matthew 27:60; Mark 15:46). It was rare to find a stone entrance to a Jewish tomb in biblical times; most Jewish tombs had doors with certain types of hinges. A large stone rolled before the tomb would be much more difficult to move, making the burial site more permanent.

However, the chief priests and Pharisees weren't so sure that the site was secure. Fearing that Jesus' disciples would come to steal the body and claim that Jesus had been resurrected, the Jewish leaders came to Pilate and said, "...Sir, we remember that that deceiver said, while he was yet alive, After three days I will rise again. Command therefore that the sepulchre be made sure until the third day, lest his disciples come by night, and steal him away, and say unto the people, He is risen from the dead: so the last error shall be worse than the first" (Matthew 27:63,64).

When the chief priests and Pharisees asked that "...the sepulchre be *made sure...*," the Greek word *sphragidzo* is used. This word described *a legal seal* that was placed on documents, letters, possessions, or, in this case, a tomb. Its purpose was *to authenticate that the sealed item had been properly inspected before sealing and that all the contents were in order.* As long as the seal remained unbroken, *it guaranteed that the contents inside were safe and sound.* In this case, the word *sphragidzo* is used to signify *the sealing of the tomb.* In all probability, it was a string that was stretched across the stone at the entrance of the tomb, which was then sealed on both sides by Pilate's legal authorities.

Before sealing the tomb, however, these authorities were first required to inspect the inside of the tomb to see that the body of Jesus was in its place. After guaranteeing that the corpse was where it was supposed to be, they rolled the stone back in place and then *sealed* it with the official seal of the governor of Rome.

After hearing the suspicions of the chief priests and Pharisees, "Pilate said unto them, Ye have a watch: go your way, make it as sure as ye can" (Matthew 27:65). The word "watch" is the Greek word *coustodia*, from which we get the word *custodian.* This was a group of four Roman soldiers whose shift changed every three hours. The changing shifts assured that the tomb would be guarded 24 hours a day by soldiers who were awake, attentive, and fully alert. When Pilate said, "Ye have a watch...," a better rendering would be, *"Here — I'm giving you a set of soldiers; take them and guard the tomb."*

Matthew 27:66 says, "So they went, and made the sepulchre sure, sealing the stone, and setting a watch." Wasting no time, the chief priests and elders hastened to the tomb with their government-issued soldiers and the special officers assigned to inspect the tomb before placing Pilate's seal upon it. After a full inspection had been made, the stone was put back in place, and the soldiers stood guard to protect the tomb from anyone who would attempt to touch it or remove its contents. Every three hours, new guards arrived to replace the old ones. These armed soldiers guarded the entrance to Jesus' tomb so firmly that *no one* would have been able to come near it.

The purpose of the seal was to authenticate that Jesus was dead; therefore, we can know that His body was thoroughly inspected again for proof of death. There is no doubt that Jesus was dead, for He was examined again and again, even as He lay in the tomb. Some critics have claimed that only Jesus' own disciples inspected His body and that they could have lied about His being dead. However, an officer from Pilate's court also examined the body of Jesus. We can also be fairly certain that the chief priests and elders who accompanied the soldiers to the burial site demanded the right to view His dead body as well so they could verify that He was truly dead.

When Jesus came out of that grave several days later, it was no hoax or fabricated story. In addition to all the people who saw Him die on the Cross, the following individuals and groups verified that His dead body was in the tomb before the stone was permanently sealed by an officer from the Roman court of law:

❖ Joseph of Arimathea carefully laid Him inside the tomb.

❖ Nicodemus provided the embalming solutions, assisted in embalming Him, and helped Joseph of Arimathea lay Him in His place in the tomb.

❖ Mary Magdalene and Mary, the mother of Joses, lovingly examined His body and carefully contemplated every aspect of the burial site to ensure everything was done properly and respectfully.

❖ Rome's official officer ordered the stone rolled back. Then he went into the tomb and examined the body of Jesus to verify that it was Jesus and that He was really dead.

❖ The chief priests and elders entered the tomb with Rome's official officer so they could look upon Jesus' dead body and put an end to their worries that He had somehow survived.

❖ Roman guards checked the contents of the tomb because they wanted to know for sure a body was there. They didn't want to be guarding an empty tomb that would later be used as a claim of resurrection, while they got blamed for the disappearance of Jesus' body.

❖ After all of these inspections were complete, Rome's official officer ordered the stone rolled back in its place. While the chief priests, elders, and Roman guards watched, he secured the site and sealed it shut with the seal of the governor of Rome.

Regardless of all these efforts to secure the site and to keep Jesus inside the grave, it was impossible for death to hold Him. When preaching on the day of Pentecost, Peter proclaimed to the people of Jerusalem, "…Ye have taken, and by wicked hands have crucified and slain [Jesus]: whom God hath raised up, having loosed the pains of death: because it was not possible that he should be holden of it" (Acts 2:23,24).

Regardless of all these efforts to secure the site and to keep Jesus inside the grave, it was impossible for death to hold Him.

Today the tomb in Jerusalem is empty because Jesus arose on the third day! Now He is seated on His throne at the right hand of the Father on High, where He ever lives to make intercession for you and for me (Hebrews 7:25). That means we never have to struggle alone. At any time of the day or night, we can come boldly before the throne of grace and ask for divine assistance (Hebrews 4:16).

There is no mountain in your life God cannot move. So make your requests known to Him, confidently expecting Him to move on your behalf. As you do, you *will* receive supernatural grace to help in time of need.

Think About It

The purpose of the seal on Jesus' tomb was to authenticate that He was indeed dead and to secure the site. Pilate's soldiers, as well as the chief priests and elders, inspected Jesus' body to verify He was truly dead.

Notice the ignorance and arrogance that led men to believe they had controlled and contained the Son of God. Are there any areas of your life that you have kept sealed and secure in an attempt to prevent God from stirring you to change?

The religious leaders recalled that Jesus said He would rise from the dead. They heard the truth but did not comprehend its significance.

Think about all that Jesus declared about Himself during His walk on this earth, and consider all He has spoken to you personally. Do you truly believe Jesus? Have you taken the time to meditate on the significance of His words?

Jesus was the Father's promise of hope for mankind. When He died and was then buried, creation was shocked and His disciples were devastated. But God raised Jesus to new life. What seemed to be the end was actually only the beginning.

Flip through the pages of your own life's story. What promise from God to you seems now incapable of coming to pass? What hope or dream in your life have you buried? Consider the power of the One who raised Jesus from the dead. Then, like Jesus, commit yourself into the hands of the One who makes all things new. He is faithful. Will you trust Him?

chapter
30
Behold, He Is Risen!

30

Behold, He Is Risen!

Jesus is *alive*!

His resurrection was not merely a philosophical renaissance of His ideas and teachings — He was literally raised from the dead!

The power of God exploded inside that tomb, reconnected Jesus' spirit with His dead body, flooded His corpse with life, and He arose! So much power was released behind the sealed entrance of His tomb that the earth itself reverberated and shuddered from the explosion. Then an angel rolled the stone from the entrance, and Jesus physically walked through the door of that tomb *alive*!

This is no legend or fairy tale. *This is the foundation of our faith!* So let's examine the events surrounding the resurrection of Jesus Christ.

He was resurrected from the dead sometime between the close of Sabbath sunset on Saturday evening and before the women came to the tomb early on Sunday morning. The only actual eyewitnesses to the resurrection itself were the angels who were present and the four Roman soldiers who had been stationed there at Pilate's command (Matthew 27:66). However, Matthew, Mark, Luke, and John all record the events that followed on the morning of His resurrection.

When you first read all four accounts of what happened that morning, it may appear that a contradiction exists between the details told in the various Gospels. But when they are chronologically aligned, the picture becomes very clear and the impression of contradiction is wiped away.

Let me give you an example of what appears to be a contradiction. The Gospel of Matthew says there was *one angel outside the tomb*. The Gospel of Mark says there was *one angel inside the tomb*. The Gospel of Luke says there were *two angels inside the tomb*. The Gospel of John says *nothing* about angels in this scene but does say that when Mary returned later in the day, she saw *two angels inside the tomb* who were positioned at the head and foot of the place where the body of Jesus had been laid.

So who is telling the right story? How many angels were there? As I said, in order to see the entire scenario that transpired that day, we have to put the events in all four Gospels in proper chronological sequence. So let's get started!

Matthew 28:1 says, "In the end of the sabbath, as it began to dawn toward the first day of the week, came Mary Magdalene and the other Mary to see the sepulchre." In addition to Mary Magdalene and the other Mary, the mother of James, Luke 24:10 tells us that "Joanna" and "other women" came to the tomb. Luke 8:3 tells us that this "Joanna" was the wife of Herod's steward — evidently a wealthy woman who was a financial supporter of Jesus' ministry. According to Luke 23:55 and 56, many of these women were present when Jesus was placed inside the tomb but returned home to prepare "spices and ointments" so they could anoint His body for burial when they returned after the Sabbath day.

These women had no way of knowing that the chief priests and elders had gone to Pilate the day after Jesus was buried to request a watch of four Roman soldiers to guard the tomb and an official from the Roman court to "seal" the tomb. *How would these women have known this?* They were at home, preparing spices and ointments.

Yet while these women were preparing to return to anoint Jesus' dead body, the tomb was being officially sealed shut and Roman soldiers had been ordered to guard the tomb 24 hours a day. Had the women known that the tomb was legally sealed and couldn't be opened, they wouldn't have returned to the tomb, for it was legally impossible for them to request the stone to be removed.

Mark 16:2-4 says, "And very early in the morning the first day of the week, they came unto the sepulchre at the rising of the sun. And they said among themselves, Who shall roll us away the stone from the door of the sepulchre? And when they looked, they saw that the stone was rolled away: for it was very great."

Ignorant of the fact that the tomb couldn't legally be opened, the women proceeded to the tomb for the purpose of anointing Jesus' body. As they drew near to the garden where the tomb was located, they wondered among themselves who would remove the stone for them. However, Matthew 28:2 says, "And, behold, there was a great earthquake...."

This earthquake didn't occur at the time when the women approached the tomb. Rather, it occurred simultaneously with the moment of Jesus' resurrection, sometime after the Saturday sunset and before the women arrived at the garden. When describing the magnitude of the earthquake, Matthew uses the word "behold." In Greek, this is the word *idou*. The *King James Version* translates it *behold*, but in our day, it might be better translated, *Wow!* This word carries the idea of *shock, amazement,* and *wonder,* so when Matthew says, "And, behold, there was a great earthquake..." he literally means, *"Wow! Can you believe it?"* The word *idou* could also carry this idea: *"Whew! Listen to the amazing thing that happened next...."* Although Matthew writes his Gospel many years after the fact, he still experiences *amazement* when he thinks of this event!

Matthew tells us that there was "a great earthquake." The word "great" is the Greek word *mega*, leaving no room for doubt as to the magnitude of this event. The word *mega* always suggests something *huge, massive,* or *enormous.* The word "earthquake" is the Greek word *seismos*, the word for *a literal earthquake*. Just as creation shook when its Creator died on the Cross, now the earth exploded with exultation at the resurrection of Jesus!

Mark 16:4 says that when the women arrived at the tomb, they found "...the stone was rolled away: for it was very great." The word "very" is the Greek word *sphodra*, meaning *very, exceedingly,* or *extremely*. The word "great" is that word *mega*, meaning *huge, massive,* or *enormous*. In other words, this was no normal stone. The authorities placed *an extremely, exceedingly massive stone* in front of the entrance to Jesus' tomb. Yet when the women arrived, it had been removed!

Matthew 28:2 tells us how the stone was removed. It says that "...the angel of the Lord descended from heaven, and came and rolled back the stone from the door, and sat upon it." The word "sat" is the Greek word *kathemai*, which means *to sit down*. Some have suggested that the ability of the angel to sit on top of such a huge stone may also denote his immense size. In other words, he was so huge that he could sit on top of the enormous stone as if it were a chair. If this were the case, the removal of the stone would have been a simple feat. Matthew informs us that not only was the angel strong, but "his countenance was like lightning, and his raiment white as snow" (v. 3).

The immense size, power, and brilliance of this angel explains why the Roman guards fled the scene. Matthew 28:4 tells us, "And for fear of him the keepers did shake, and became as dead men." The word "fear" is the Greek word *phobos*, which means *to fear*. In this case, it was such a *panic-stricken fear* that it caused the guards to "shake."

This word "shake" is derived from the Greek word *seio*, the identical root word for an *earthquake*. The mighty Roman soldiers trembled and quaked at the sight of the angel. In fact, they "...became as dead men." The words "dead men" is the Greek word *nekros* — the word for *a corpse*. The soldiers were so terrified at the appearance of the angel that they fell to the ground, violently trembling and so paralyzed with fear that they were unable to move. When they were finally able to move again, these guards fled the scene — and when the women arrived at the garden, they were nowhere to be found!

Luke 24:3 tells us that with the stone removed, these women passed right by the angel who sat on top of the huge stone and crossed the threshold into the tomb. It says, "And they entered in, and found not the body of the Lord Jesus." *But what did they find inside the tomb besides the vacant spot where Jesus had laid?* Mark 16:5 tells us: "And entering into the sepulchre, they saw a young man sitting on the right side, clothed in a long white garment; and they were affrighted."

First, these women saw an angel sitting on top of the stone at the entrance of the tomb. Now inside the tomb, they see another angel whose appearance is like a young man. The words "young man" are from the Greek word *neanikos*, referring to *a young man who is filled with vigor and energy and who is in the prime of his life*. This illustrates the *vitality*, *strength*, and *ever-youthful appearance* of angels. The Bible also tells us that this angel was "...clothed in a long white garment...." The word "clothed" pictures *a garment draped about his shoulders*, as a mighty warrior or ruler would be dressed. The word "garment" is from the Greek word *stole*, which represents *the long, flowing robe that adorned royalty, commanders, kings, priests, and other people of high distinction*.

As these women stood in an empty tomb, Luke 24:4 tells us that "...they were much perplexed thereabout...." This Greek word for "perplexed" is *aporeo*, which means *to lose one's way*. It is the picture of someone who is so confused that he can't figure out where he is, what he's doing, or what is happening around him. This person is completely *bewildered* by surrounding events.

Of course these women were perplexed! They came expecting to see the stone in front of the tomb, but it was *removed*. Sitting on top of the massive stone was *a dazzling angel*. To get into the tomb, they had to pass by that angel — but once in the tomb, they discovered there was *no dead body*. Then suddenly they looked over to the right side of the tomb and saw *a second angel*, dressed in a long, white robe like a warrior, ruler, priest, or king. The women didn't expect to encounter any of these unusual events that morning. It would have been normal for their heads to be whirling with questions!

Then Luke 24:4 tells us that all of a sudden "...two men stood by them in shining garments." The words "stood by" are from the Greek word *epistemi*, which means *to come upon suddenly*; *to take one by surprise*; *to burst upon the scene*; *to suddenly step up*; or *to unexpectedly appear*. In other words, while the women tried to figure out what they were seeing, the angel sitting on top of the stone decided to join the group inside the tomb. Suddenly to the women's amazement, *two* angels were standing inside the tomb in "shining garments"!

The word "shining" is *astrapto*, depicting something that *shines* or *flashes like lightning*. It may refer to the angels' shining appearance.

Luke 24:5-8 says, "And as they were afraid, and bowed down their faces to the earth, they [the angels] said unto them, Why seek ye the living among the dead? He is not here, but is risen: remember how he spake unto you when he was yet in Galilee, saying, The Son of man must be delivered into the hands of sinful men, and be crucified, and the third day rise again. And they remembered his words."

After the two angels proclaimed the joyful news of Jesus' resurrection, they instructed the women, "But go your way, tell his disciples and Peter that he goeth before you into Galilee: there shall ye see him, as he said unto you" (Mark 16:7). Matthew 28:8 says they "...did run to bring his disciples word." Mark 16:8 says, "And they went out quickly, and fled from the sepulchre...." Luke 24:9,10 says that the women returned and "...told these things unto the apostles."

Can you imagine how flustered these women must have been as they tried to tell the apostles what they had seen and heard that morning? Luke 24:11 says, "And their words seemed to them as idle tales, and they believed them not." The words "idle tales" are from the Greek word *leros*, which means *nonsense*, *idle talk*, *babble*, or *delirium*. In other words, the women's presentation of the Gospel probably wasn't extremely clear, but it stirred enough interest in Peter and John to make them get up and go find out for themselves about Jesus!

When we've had a supernatural encounter with the Lord, it isn't always easy to put that experience into words. This is a frustration all of us who know the Lord have felt at one time or another. However, we can't let that keep us from spreading the good news of what Jesus Christ has done in our lives. We should never forget that although these women seemed to be babbling and speaking nonsense, their words were all that was needed to spark an interest in those men and compel them to get up and go find out about Jesus themselves.

The women's presentation of the Gospel probably wasn't extremely clear, but it stirred enough interest in Peter and John to make them get up and go find out for themselves about Jesus!

As you share Jesus Christ with your family and friends, it is your job to "give it your best shot." Tell the Good News the best way you know how! But don't overlook the fact that the Holy Spirit is also speaking to their hearts at the same time you are speaking to their ears. The Spirit of God will use you and your witness to stir hunger deep in their hearts. But long after you are finished talking, God will still be dealing with them. And when they come to Jesus, they won't remember if you sounded confusing the day you presented the Gospel to them. They will be thankful that you loved them enough to care for their souls!

So get up and get going! Open your mouth, and start telling the Good News that Jesus Christ is alive and well!

Think About It

The resurrection is the foundation of the Christian faith. Jesus Christ who was dead is now alive forevermore (Revelation 1:18). The One who conquered death, hell, and the grave is seated at the right hand of the Father, interceding right now for you and for all that concerns you. Think about that!

Just as the earth quaked when its Creator died on the Cross, the earth exploded with exultation when Jesus was raised from the dead by the glory of God the Father. Now creation is waiting for you to walk in the reality of the victory Jesus purchased for you with His own blood. Consider the significance of that truth in light of the choices you make on a daily basis.

The most determined efforts of men under demonic influence could not prevent the power of God from restoring Jesus to life.

What is the greatest obstacle or difficulty in your life? If you are born again, the same Spirit who raised Jesus from the dead dwells in you. Think about what that divine power could do for you if you'd allow the Holy Spirit to have access to the "dead" situations in your life.

chapter

31

An Empty Tomb

31

An Empty Tomb

By the time the women reached the apostles, they must have sounded very *confused*! On one hand, the women reported that the angels said Jesus was alive from the dead. On the other hand, they were confused and operating in fear, so they exclaimed, "...They have taken away the Lord out of the sepulchre, and we know not where they have laid him" (John 20:2).

Fear always produces confusion, and these women were so confused that the apostles didn't take what they said seriously. Luke 24:11 says, "And their words seemed to them as idle tales, and they believed them not." As we saw earlier, the words "idle tales" are from the Greek word *leros*, which means *nonsense*, *idle talk*, *babble*, or *delirium*. Who did these women think removed Jesus from the tomb? Which story was true? Was He resurrected and alive as the women first told the apostles, or was He stolen away?

John 20:3,4 says, "Peter therefore went forth, and that other disciple, and came to the sepulchre. So they ran both together: and the other disciple [John] did outrun Peter, and came first to the sepulchre." When the Bible says Peter and John "went forth," the Greek tense indicates that their feet were moving before the conversation with the women concluded. When they heard that something had happened at the tomb, both men were on the move to get there as quickly as possible.

We also know from John 20:11 that Mary Magdalene soon followed Peter and John back to the tomb, for she was present at the site and remained there after Peter and John returned to the apostles.

I find it interesting that when Peter and John raced to the tomb to see whatever it was that the women were trying to communicate to them, none of the other apostles joined them. The others apparently just sat and watched Peter and John put on their clothes and start running, but they didn't join the two men. Instead, the rest of the apostles probably stayed behind to discuss what they had heard and to debate about what it meant.

Because Peter and John ran to the garden, they experienced something the other apostles missed by staying home. *It is simply a fact that if you want to experience Jesus Christ and His power, you must get up from where you are and start moving in His direction.*

John outran Peter to the garden where the tomb was located. As soon as John arrived, John 20:5 tells us, "And he stooping down, and looking in, saw the linen clothes lying; yet went he not in." The Greek word for "stooping down" is *parakupto*. It means *to peer into*; *to peep into*; *to bend low to take a closer look*; or *to stoop down to see something better*.

> *It is simply a fact that if you want to experience Jesus Christ and His power, you must get up from where you are and start moving in His direction.*

John bent down so he could take a close peek into the tomb, and he "...saw the linen clothes lying...." The word "saw" is the Greek word *blepo*, which means *to see*. It was just enough of a *glance* to see the linen clothes lying there. The words "linen clothes" is the same identical word used in John 19:40 when referring to the expensive Egyptian-made garment in which Joseph of Arimathea and Nicodemus had buried Jesus (the Greek word *othonion*; *see* Chapter 28). If Jesus had been stolen, whoever took Him would have taken this expensive garment as well, but John saw that these linen clothes had been left lying in the tomb.

Graves were a place of respect for the Jews, which may explain the reason John was hesitant to enter the tomb. It is also quite possible that he observed the broken seals and realized that it looked like an unlawful entry had occurred. Perhaps he was thinking twice before he found himself connected to an alleged potential crime scene. Regardless of why John hesitated, the Bible tells us that Peter did *not* hesitate but promptly barged right into the tomb to check it out for himself: "Then cometh Simon Peter following him, and went into the sepulchre, and seeth the linen clothes lie, and the napkin, that was about his head, not lying with the linen clothes, but wrapped together in a place by itself" (John 20:6,7).

John only glanced into the interior of the tomb, but the above verse says Peter went into the sepulcher and "...seeth the linen clothes lie." The word "seeth" is the Greek word *theaomai*, from which we get our word *theater*. It means *to fully see* or *fully observe*, like a patron who carefully watches every act of a play at the theater.

When Peter entered that tomb, he surveyed it like a professional surveyor. He looked over every nook and cranny, paying special attention to the linen clothes and the way they were left there. He saw "...the napkin, that was about his head, not lying with the linen clothes, but wrapped together in a place by itself." The word "napkin" is *soudarion*, and it refers to *a napkin that could be used for wiping perspiration from one's face*. This word was also used in connection with *a burial cloth that was gently placed upon the face of the dead at burial*.

When Lazarus came out of the tomb, Jesus instructed that Lazarus' grave clothes be removed along with the *soudarion*, or napkin, from his face (John 11:44). Apparently Jesus' entire body was wrapped in a large white linen sheet, but His face was covered with such a napkin in traditional Jewish burial style.

The most fascinating fact about this facial cloth was that it was "...wrapped together in a place by itself." The word "wrapped" is the Greek word *entulisso*, which means *to neatly fold*; *to nicely arrange*; or *to arrange in an orderly fashion*. The reason this word is so interesting is that it tells us Jesus was calm and completely in control of His faculties when He was raised from the dead. He removed the expensive Egyptian-made burial cloth from His body, sat upright, and then removed the burial napkin from His face. Sitting in that upright position, He neatly folded the burial cloth and gently laid it down to one side, separate from the linen clothes He probably laid down on His other side. Now as Peter gazed at the scene inside the tomb, he could see the empty spot where Jesus had sat between these two pieces of burial clothing after He was raised from the dead.

John 20:8 says, "Then went in also that other disciple, which came first to the sepulchre, and he saw, and believed." This verse says that when John saw the empty stone slab where Jesus' body had previously lain and the burial clothes lying to the right and to the left, forming the empty spot where Jesus sat after He was resurrected, John then "believed." I find it truly amazing that even though Peter had spent a longer time than John inside the tomb, he was still uncertain as to the meaning of it all. Luke 24:12 says that Peter "…departed, wondering in himself at that which was come to pass." John, on the other hand, left the tomb believing Jesus was alive.

Later that evening, Jesus would appear to all the apostles and breathe the Spirit of God into them, giving them the new birth (John 20:22). But at this moment, because the Holy Spirit was not yet resident in them as their Teacher, there was much they could not understand. Even though Jesus had told them He would die and be raised from the dead, they simply were not yet able to comprehend it. That's why John 20:9 says, "For as yet they knew not the scripture, that he must rise again from the dead."

Although the apostles had heard this scripture from Jesus Himself, the reality and full impact of its truth had not registered in their hearts. After this historical and momentous day, the Bible tells us, "Then the disciples went away again unto their own home" (v. 10).

It is remarkable to me that Peter could stand in the middle of Jesus' empty tomb and still leave uncertain about what it meant. How in the world would it be possible to be in the very room where Jesus' dead body had lain, to see the neatly folded napkin, to recognize the spot where He sat upright between those garments, and to still not be able to figure out that Jesus was now alive?

Yet it starts making sense when I think about it. God has done so many unquestionable miracles for you and me as well. How many times have we walked away unaffected by the power and miracles we've seen and experienced? God has delivered us, saved us, and rescued us from harm time and time again; yet we still tend to wonder if God is really with us or not. How in the world could we ever question the faithfulness of God after all He has already done for us?

We need to make sure we don't remain unmoved and unchanged by the miracle-working power of God that has already worked in our lives in the past. Instead, we should make the decision to fully embrace every good thing God has done for us — to acknowledge His work in our lives so entirely that it changes our outlook on life and transforms us from the inside out. God is good! He has been good to every one of us. If we fail to remember this, it is only because we're not opening our eyes to see His hand of protection, provision, and safety all around us.

Make a conscious choice to recognize all that God has done and is continuing to do in your life. Then remember to thank Him for it, and determine never to forget His faithfulness to perfect all that concerns you as you trust in Him.

Think About It

Peter and John were both fervent in their love for Jesus, yet always radically different in their responses to Him.

How do you respond to Jesus in worship, in prayer, and in your daily life? What do your responses reveal about your devotion and obedience to Jesus?

Everything about the scene in the empty sepulcher was orderly. When Jesus removed His burial garment, He neatly folded the facial cloth and set it aside. In Pilate's court, on Golgotha's hill, in the garden tomb, Jesus maintained a focused presence of mind. He always *acted* and never *reacted*.

Is self-composure a trait that you would attribute to yourself? What evidence in your life can you give to support your answer?

Have you ever experienced the miracle power of God? If so, how did that affect you? Does the memory of it still leave you with a sense of awe, or has time (or cynicism) dimmed your fervor and affection for God and dulled your appreciation for His goodness?

chapter

32

The First Woman Preacher

When Peter and John left the garden, Mary Magdalene remained behind. She had followed the two men, possibly hoping to obtain a clearer understanding of what she had experienced that day. All she knew was that her day started with a desire to come to the tomb to anoint the body of Jesus. But when she arrived, the stone was rolled away and an angel was sitting on top of the great stone (Matthew 28:2)! Then when she entered the tomb, she first discovered another angel (Mark 16:5) and then suddenly found herself in the presence of *two* angels inside the tomb (Luke 24:4)!

The angels had told Mary, "He is not here, but is risen…" (Luke 24:6). *But if Jesus was risen as the angels had said, where was He? How could she find Him?*

Feeling dejected and alone, Mary stood outside the tomb weeping. The Greek tense means *continually weeping*, highlighting the fact she was extremely troubled about the inexplicable events that were happening. Most of all, she wanted to know what had happened to Jesus. John writes, "…She stooped down, and looked into the sepulchre" (John 20:11). The word "stooped down" is *parakupto*, the same word used in John 20:5 to portray John taking a *peek into* the tomb. Now it was Mary's turn to bend low and peer into the empty sepulcher — but when she looked inside, she saw something she didn't expect!

John tells us, "…She stooped down, and looked into the sepulchre, and seeth two angels in white sitting, the one at the head, and the other at the feet, where the body of Jesus had lain" (John 20:11,12). The word "seeth" is the Greek word *theaomai*, which tells us assuredly that Mary *fixed her eyes* on the angels and *determined to look them over and to take in the whole experience*. First, she saw that the two angels were "in white." This agrees with all the other experiences of angels that eventful day. All of them had been dressed in shining white with a lightning-bright appearance. All the angels seen that day also wore the same type of robe — like the long, flowing regal robes worn by warriors, kings, priests, or any other person of great power and authority. The usage of the word *theaomai* ("seeth") tells us that this time Mary *visibly studied* every single detail of the angels she saw in the tomb.

John goes on to inform us that Mary saw these angels "…sitting, the one at the head, and the other at the feet, where the body of Jesus had lain." This statement is in perfect agreement with the interior of a rock-hewn tomb during biblical times. Past the entrance of such a tomb, a smaller separate room with a table-shaped pedestal, also carved from stone, was usually located to one side. On this rock slab the body was laid to rest after being dressed in burial clothes and perfumed by loved ones. The head would be slightly elevated, causing the trunk of the corpse to lie in a sloping downward position with the feet resting against a small ledge or in a groove, either of which was designed to keep the body from slipping from the slab.

When Mary saw the angels, she noted that one was seated at the top of the burial slab and the other was seated at the foot. In between these angels, she could see the empty place where she had personally viewed Jesus several days earlier. Luke 23:55 tells us that after Jesus' body was placed in the tomb, Mary Magdalene and other women who came from Galilee "…beheld the sepulchre, and how his body was laid."

The word "beheld" (*theaomai*) means *to gaze upon, to fully see*, or *to look at intently*. These women *inspected* the tomb, *gazing upon* the dead body of Jesus *to see* that it had been honorably laid in place. Because Mark 15:47 uses the imperfect tense to tell us how the women looked upon

Jesus' dead body, it means these women took plenty of time to make certain He was properly laid there. Now Mary saw the same spot where she had so carefully labored days before, but the dead body she cherished was no longer there.

As Mary looked and wept, the angels asked her, "…Woman, why weepest thou? She saith unto them, Because they have taken away my Lord, and I know not where they have laid him. And when she had thus said, she turned herself back, and saw Jesus standing, and knew not that it was Jesus" (John 20:13,14).

Stricken with sorrow, Mary withdrew from the tomb just in time to see a Man standing nearby. Due to Jesus' changed appearance, she was unable to recognize Him. Verse 15 tells us what happened next: "Jesus saith unto her, Woman, why weepest thou? whom seekest thou? She, supposing him to be the gardener, saith unto him, Sir, if thou have borne him hence, tell me where thou hast laid him, and I will take him away."

At that very moment, Jesus tenderly said, "Mary." Upon hearing that voice and recognizing the old familiar way in which He called her name, "…she turned herself, and saith unto him, Rabboni; which is to say, Master" (v. 16). Although Jesus' appearance was different now, Mary knew Him by His voice. This reminds me of John 10:27, when Jesus told His disciples, "My sheep hear my voice…." Mary knew His voice and recognized that it was her Shepherd who stood before her.

In Revelation 1, John tells us about his vision on the island of Patmos. In the midst of this phenomenal divine visitation, he says, "I was in the Spirit on the Lord's day, and heard behind me a great voice, as of a trumpet…. and I turned to see the voice that spake with me…" (Revelation 1:10,12). Like Mary, when John heard that voice, he recognized it as the voice of Jesus. This is why John writes, "…I turned to see the voice that spake with me."

Of course, it is impossible to "see" a voice, but John recognized the sound of that voice and turned to match the face with the voice he heard.

He knew it was Jesus. But as Mary had also discovered, Jesus' physical appearance looked radically different from the Jesus whom John had known in His earthly form. But the voice of Jesus never changed, and John immediately recognized it.

It appears that Mary reached out to cling to Jesus with her hands, but Jesus forbade her, saying, "…Touch me not; for I am not yet ascended unto my Father: but go to my brethren, and say unto them, I ascend unto my Father, and your Father; and to my God, and your God" (John 20:17). With this one statement, Jesus let it be known that everything had changed because of the Cross. *Now a new relationship with God was available to the apostles and to all who would call upon the name of Jesus Christ!*

Jesus let it be known that everything had changed because of the Cross. Now a new relationship with God was available to the apostles and to all who would call upon the name of Jesus Christ!

John 20:18 goes on to say, "Mary Magdalene came and told the disciples that she had seen the Lord, and that he had spoken these things unto her." In telling the disciples about her experience with the risen Lord, Mary became the first woman preacher of the Gospel!

Today we rejoice that Jesus is alive! Because of what He did for us at the Cross, now we have access to God the Father. This was the purpose of the Cross: To redeem mankind and to put man back in right relationship and fellowship with his Heavenly Father. Jesus paid it all! He finished the work of redemption so that today we can be in right relationship with God by accepting the work of Christ on Calvary by faith.

I encourage you to be bold in recognizing the voice of Jesus. If you belong to Him, then you do know His voice. Mary knew His voice; John knew His voice; and your born-again spirit knows His voice as well. If you'll take the time to listen, you will hear the voice of Jesus calling out to you, just as He tenderly called out to Mary that day in the garden. He knows you by name, and He wants to enjoy close fellowship with you. If you'll take the time to listen, you will come to know Jesus better than any other person in your life, and He will be faithful to guide you with divine accuracy through every challenging situation you face.

Think About It

Although Mary didn't recognize the risen Jesus when she first saw Him, the moment He said her name, she recognized His voice. Do you remember a time when you were acutely aware that Jesus had called you by name? How did you respond, and what was the outcome of that experience?

Notice that the very first person Jesus commissioned to proclaim the news of His resurrection was a woman. In the Garden of Eden, a woman operating under deception disobeyed and thus aided the fall of mankind. In the garden of the resurrection, a woman empowered by revelation obeyed and thus carried the news of man's redemption and restoration.

In what ways are you being obedient to proclaim to others the Good News of what Jesus has done?

When Jesus said to Mary, "I ascend unto My Father and your Father, to My God and your God," He declared that as surely as He was raised to new life, mankind was lifted to a new level as well.

If you believe in Jesus and His sacrifice for you, God is your Father and your God. How have you allowed that truth to shape your identity and influence the way you respond to God in matters big and small?

chapter
33

Eyewitness Accounts That Jesus Rose From the Dead

chapter

33

Eyewitness Accounts That Jesus Rose From the Dead

On Resurrection Day itself, Jesus appeared to the disciples at various times and places. It was simply a physical impossibility for Him to be at so many different places in one day. These appearances therefore revealed that Jesus' glorified body didn't have the same limitations His earthly body possessed before His resurrection and glorification. The Bible makes it plain that in His glorified condition, He was able to appear, to disappear, to travel great distances, and to even supernaturally pass through a wall or the locked door of a house (John 20:26).

On the same day Jesus was raised from the dead, He not only appeared to Mary Magdalene outside the garden tomb (John 20:14-17), but to two disciples as they walked from Jerusalem to the city of Emmaus (Luke 24:13-31). When the three men sat down to eat together, Jesus blessed the food. After hearing the way He blessed the food, the two disciples instantly recognized it was the Lord — just as He suddenly "...vanished out of their sight" (v. 31).

That same evening, Jesus supernaturally traveled through the walls of a house where the 11 disciples were gathered, miraculously appearing right in front of them. John 20:19 tells us about this amazing event: "Then the same day at evening, being the first day of the week, when the doors were shut where the disciples were assembled for fear of the Jews...."

This verse says that when the disciples gathered for dinner, they made certain "the doors were shut." The word "door" is *thura*, which lets us know this was a door that was *large* and *solid*. But as if this were not enough, the verse tells us that these doors "were shut."

The word "shut" is the Greek word *kleio*, meaning *locked*. Doors of this kind were usually locked with a heavy bolt that slid through rings attached to the door and the frame — like the deadbolts we use in doors today, only heavier. This door would be difficult, if not impossible, to break down. The fact that it was locked "for fear of the Jews" tells us that the disciples had moved into a mode of self-preservation and protection.

With rumors of Jesus' resurrection already filling the city of Jerusalem, there was no certainty that the leaders who crucified Jesus wouldn't try to arrest the rest of the apostles and do the same to them as they had to Jesus. We know that the Roman guards who fled the resurrection site "...shewed unto the chief priests all the things that were done" (Matthew 28:11). To prevent the people of Israel from knowing the truth of Jesus' resurrection, the chief priests and elders bribed the soldiers to keep their mouths shut about what they had seen. Verse 12 tells us, "And when they were assembled with the elders, and had taken counsel, they gave large money unto the soldiers."

The chief priests and elders fabricated a story and told the soldiers what they were to say when people asked them what happened: "...Say ye, His disciples came by night, and stole him away while we slept" (v. 13).

The soldiers' admission that they had slept on the job would deem them worthy of punishment in Pilate's sight, so the religious leaders further assured them, "And if this come to the governor's ears, we will persuade him, and secure you" (v. 14). The soldiers listened to the religious leaders' plan and were satisfied with the amount of money being offered to them to keep silent. Verse 15 then says, "So they took the money, and did as they were taught...."

Once the chief priests and elders had bought the testimony of the Roman guards, they were positioned to make some serious arrests. First, we know that they were already asserting that the disciples had stolen the body of Jesus. But to steal the body, they had to either overpower the Roman guards or creep past them as they slept. Either way, this would be deemed a terrible dishonor to the guards' reputation. And if the disciples were caught, they'd potentially be put to death for this action.

To open the tomb, the governor's seal had to be broken. Breaking that seal was an offense that required the death sentence, for this was a breach of the empire's power. No doubt the same angry mobs that cheered while Jesus carried His crossbeam to Golgotha were still in the city. The city was already in turmoil due to such strange happenings — the sky turning dark in the middle of the day with no natural explanation; the veil of the temple rent in half; the various earthquakes shaking the entire surrounding territory. It wouldn't take too much to put the whole city on edge and turn them against the disciples. This is why the disciples were locked behind closed doors that evening.

But although the doors were sealed tightly shut, Jesus supernaturally passed right through solid matter and appeared in the midst of the disciples. John 20:19 says Jesus came "…and stood in the midst, and saith unto them, Peace be unto you."

No doubt this sudden appearance must have terrified the disciples. Luke 24:37 tells us that "…they were terrified and affrighted, and supposed that they had seen a spirit." This is why Jesus told them, "…Why are ye troubled? and why do thoughts arise in your hearts? Behold my hands and my feet, that it is I myself: handle me, and see; for a spirit hath not flesh and bones, as ye see me have" (vv. 38,39).

Notice Jesus said, "Handle me." This is the Greek word *psilaphao*, and it literally means *to touch*, *to squeeze*, or *to feel*. Jesus gave the disciples permission to examine His resurrected body to see that it was a real body and not a spirit.

All of a sudden Jesus asked them, "...Have ye here any meat?" The following verses say, "And they gave him a piece of a broiled fish, and of an honeycomb. And he took it, and did eat before them" (Luke 24:42,43). After eating the fish and honeycomb, Jesus began to speak to them from the Scriptures, pointing out key Old Testament prophecies having to do with Him. Luke 24:45 says, "Then opened he their understanding, that they might understand the scriptures." Jesus explained to the disciples that repentance would have to be preached in His name among all the nations, but that it was to begin in Jerusalem. This is when He told them, "...As my Father hath sent me, even so send I you" (John 20:21).

The disciple Thomas had not been present in the room that night when Jesus passed through solid matter and entered into the room. Later that evening Thomas joined them and heard the news, but by that time Jesus was already gone. He scoffed at the other disciples and said, "...Except I shall see in his hands the print of the nails, and put my finger into the print of the nails, and thrust my hand into his side, I will not believe" (John 20:25).

Eight days later, the disciples were behind locked doors again, but this time Thomas was with them. John 20:26,27 says, "...Then came Jesus, the doors being shut, and stood in the midst, and said, Peace be unto you. Then saith he to Thomas, Reach hither thy finger, and behold my hands; and reach hither thy hand, and thrust it into my side: and be not faithless, but believing." Of course, after this event, Thomas believed!

Jesus appeared to His disciples again, this time at the Sea of Tiberias. Peter, Thomas Didymus, Nathanael, the sons of Zebedee, and two other disciples followed Peter to the seacoast to go fishing. But after fishing all night, the disciples had caught nothing.

Then in the morning, Jesus stood on the shore and called to the disciples to cast their nets on the other side of the boat. Although they weren't sure who was instructing them, the men obeyed anyway — and caught so many fish that they weren't even able to pull their nets into the boat! That's when they recognized that the Man who had instructed them was the Lord (John 21:2-7).

Before the evening was finished, Jesus had sat around a campfire with them, eaten fish with them, and spent time fellowshipping with them. John 21:14 says, "This is now the third time that Jesus shewed himself to his disciples, after that he was risen from the dead."

Then finally, the disciples gathered together on the same mountain in Galilee where Jesus had first ordained them. He appeared to them there and gave them the Great Commission. He told them, "...All power is given unto me in heaven and in earth. Go ye therefore, and teach all nations, baptizing them in the name of the Father, and of the Son, and of the Holy Ghost: teaching them to observe all things whatsoever I have commanded you: and, lo, I am with you alway, even unto the end of the world. Amen" (Matthew 28:18-20).

In addition to these appearances recorded in the Gospels, First Corinthians 15:5-7 says, "And that he was seen of Cephas, then of the twelve: after that, he was seen of above five hundred brethren at once; of whom the greater part remain unto this present, but some are fallen asleep. After that, he was seen of James; then of all the apostles." Acts 1:3 says, "...He shewed himself alive after his passion by many infallible proofs, being seen of them forty days, and speaking of the things pertaining to the kingdom of God."

The resurrected Jesus drew near to His disciples — but do you draw near to Him as you go about the activities of your daily life?

How about you? Do you experience Jesus Christ in the daily activities of your life, or is Jesus just relegated to church services and Sunday school? From what you just read, you now know that Jesus was "in the midst" of His disciples after His resurrection. They ate with Him, talked to Him, and fellowshipped with Him. Jesus even helped them catch fish! The resurrected

Jesus drew near to His disciples — but do you draw near to Him as you go about the activities of your daily life?

Even though Jesus is seated right now at the right hand of the Father on High, you can know Him intimately through the ministry of the Holy Spirit. The Holy Spirit is the Great Revealer of Jesus Christ. Just ask the Holy Spirit to show you Jesus, and He will be faithful to make Jesus more real to you than your natural mind can even imagine.

Think About It

Jesus chided Thomas for not believing until he saw. At the same time, Jesus pronounced a blessing on all who would believe He had risen from the dead without actually having seen Him.

The Person of the Holy Spirit is a Revealer. It is His role to not only show you things to come, but also to show you, in increasing depth and clarity, who Jesus is both *to* you and *through* you as a member of His Body on the earth. Are you taking the time to fellowship with God so the Holy Spirit can give you the revelation that you need and that your heart desires?

Did you ever wish you could have walked with Jesus when He was on the earth? If so, you're actually longing for less than what is available to you right now. Through the written Word of God and the ministry of the Holy Spirit, you can actually experience an even closer, more intimate fellowship with Jesus than His disciples shared with Him during His earthly ministry.

Scriptures describe the strength and exploits demonstrated in the lives of those who walked with Jesus. Think about what God can accomplish through *your* life as you consciously choose to walk daily with Jesus via His Word and His Spirit.

Jesus told His disciples that when they saw Him, they saw the Father (John 14:7). Can the same be said of you?

If you're a Christian, you are to be Jesus' representative on the earth, reflecting His nature and His ways. When people reach out to you, do they sense Jesus reaching back to them through you? In what ways do you deliberately give witness to the fact that Jesus is alive in you?

chapter

34

*What Has Jesus Been Doing
for the Past 2,000 Years?*

34

What Has Jesus Been Doing for the Past 2,000 Years?

When Luke wrote Acts chapter 1, he chronicled events in the final days of Jesus' appearance on earth. He says that Jesus "...shewed himself alive after his passion by many infallible proofs, being seen of them forty days, and speaking of the things pertaining to the kingdom of God" (v. 3). In Acts 1:9, Luke goes on to tell us that at the end of those 40 days after Jesus had spoken to His followers one final time, "...he was taken up; and a cloud received him out of their sight."

Luke continues, "And while they [the apostles] looked stedfastly toward heaven as he went up, behold, two men stood by them in white apparel; which also said, Ye men of Galilee, why stand ye gazing up into heaven? this same Jesus, which is taken up from you into heaven, shall so come in like manner as ye have seen him go into heaven" (Acts 1:10,11). On that day, the angels declared Jesus would return in the same manner He left nearly 2,000 years ago.

Days later when Peter preached his first message on the Day of Pentecost, he declared that Jesus would remain in Heaven until the fulfillment of all Scripture at the end of the age (*see* Acts 3:21). Only when every prophecy as yet unfulfilled has finally been fulfilled will Jesus return — and when He does return, it will be exactly in the same way He ascended nearly 2,000 years ago. However, this time Jesus won't return as a humble Servant. The Bible declares that He will return as the King of kings and the Lord of lords!

When the disciples watched Jesus ascend into a cloud of glory that received Him into Heaven, it was the last time Jesus was ever seen on earth in His physical human form. Of course, since that time, people have experienced supernatural moments when they've seen Jesus in the Spirit, whether in visions or in dreams. And we also know that Jesus is touching people's lives today through His Church, which Scripture even refers to as the *Body* of Christ.

But Jesus Himself — in His actual physical form — left the earth 2,000 years ago, and He has been absent ever since. And He will remain absent until every scripture related to the last days has been fulfilled. Although we may try to predict when that day will come and may even be able to recognize the reason for Jesus' second coming, Matthew 24:36 tells us that only the Father knows the exact day and hour when Jesus will return.

When Peter preached on the Day of Pentecost, he told his listening audience where Jesus was at that moment: Having ascended to Heaven, Jesus was sitting at the Father's right hand! Peter then declared that once Jesus was seated in His new permanent position at the Father's right hand, His first order of business was to pour out the gift of the Holy Spirit upon the Church (*see* Acts 2:33). That is *exactly* what happened on the Day of Pentecost.

In Acts 2:1 and 2, the Bible tells us, "And when the day of Pentecost was fully come, they [the 120 disciples who gathered in the Upper Room in Jerusalem] were all with one accord in one place. And suddenly there came a sound from heaven as of a rushing mighty wind, and it filled all the house where they were sitting."

The rushing mighty wind heard on the Day of Pentecost was the supernatural sound of the Holy Spirit's descent and entrance into the Church that initiated the Church Age and the Dispensation of the Holy Spirit. The words "rushing wind" come from a Greek word that was normally used to describe *an ear-deafening crash* or *the roar of the waves of the sea, especially during winter storms.*

Have you ever been near the sea during a winter storm and heard the crashing roar of the waves? It's so loud that you can hardly hear another person speak — even if he's standing alongside you.

This categorically tells us that when the Holy Spirit made His entrance on the Day of Pentecost, it was no quiet affair. It was loud, noisy, thunderous, and boisterous. Although the Holy Spirit is a Gentleman, He isn't afraid of a loud noise.

The truth is, the entrance of the Third Person of the Trinity was so vociferous that every person present on the Day of Pentecost understood that the Holy Spirit had descended, just as Jesus prophesied (*see* John 14:16). Ever since that time the Holy Spirit has been on the earth to represent and glorify Jesus and to empower believers to do the works of Jesus.

These past 2,000 years — and as long as the Church Age exists — have been and will be the *Dispensation of the Holy Spirit*. As wonderful as this Dispensation is, all of our hearts long for that day when the clouds will roll back and Jesus Himself once again will descend into the world. But until that time when Jesus suddenly and supernaturally appears, this is and will remain the age when the Holy Spirit is at work as Jesus' Representative in the world. This is why we must do everything we can to learn more about the Holy Spirit and how to partner with Him in this life.

Since this is the Dispensation of the Holy Spirit and Jesus Himself has been physically absent from the earth since the day He ascended into Heaven, where is Jesus now and what has He been doing for the last 2,000 years?

When Jesus' feet lifted from the earth and He was received into Heaven, Hebrews 8:6 tells us that He started the next phase of His ministry — a phase so wonderful that this verse calls it "…*a more excellent ministry*, by how much also he is the mediator of a better covenant, which was established upon better promises."

The Greek word for "excellent" means *incomparable, unparalleled, unsurpassed, unmatched, finest, greatest*, or *most excellent*. This means Jesus' present-day ministry is *not even to be compared* to His previous earthly ministry. In fact, Hebrews 8:6 emphatically lets us know that Jesus' ministry in this Dispensation of the Holy Spirit is His *finest, greatest*, and *most excellent* ministry.

Why is this phase of Jesus' ministry so excellent?

What is He doing right now that is so mighty?

The moment Jesus sat down at the Father's right hand, His ministry was initiated as the Great High Priest to everyone who calls on His name. Under the Old Covenant, there were many priests, but each of them eventually died due to their human condition. However, Hebrews 7:24,25 declares, "But this man [Jesus], because he continueth ever, hath an unchangeable priesthood. Wherefore he is able also to save them to the uttermost that come unto God by him, seeing that he ever liveth to make intercession for them."

Hebrews 4:15,16 also describes the power of Jesus' present-day ministry: "For we have not an high priest which cannot be touched with the feeling of our infirmities; but was in all points tempted like as we are, yet without sin. Let us therefore come boldly unto the throne of grace, that we may obtain mercy, and find grace to help in time of need."

This is the best news you've ever heard! Think of it — Jesus has become your Great High Priest — your personal Representative who sits at the right hand of the Father in Heaven. His ministry today is to represent *you* to the Father.

Jesus' ministry today is to represent you to the Father. And because Jesus lived on earth as a Man, He understands every problem or temptation that will ever come your way.

And because Jesus lived on earth as a Man, He understands every problem or temptation that will ever come your way.

Jesus has faced every temptation that any human being has ever encountered in life. This means He has experienced every temptation *you* face. Anything you talk to Jesus about is something that He was personally tempted with when He walked the earth and that He personally understands. But the Bible declares that although He was tempted in all ways just as we are, Jesus was without sin. Therefore, He is qualified today to sit at the Father's right hand and intercede on our behalf.

This is why Hebrews 4:16 tells us, "Let us therefore come boldly unto the throne of grace, that we may obtain mercy, and find grace to help in time of need." The word "boldly" comes from the often-used Greek word *parresia*, which refers to *freedom of speech*. It presents the picture of a person who *speaks his mind* and who does it *straightforwardly* and with great *confidence*.

Frequently in New Testament times, the word *parresia* depicted a *frankness* that was so *bold*, it was regularly met with resistance, hostility, and opposition. It just wasn't acceptable to speak so candidly. Therefore, when someone spoke his mind and his thoughts this freely, his outspokenness was met with rebuke time and time again.

But the Holy Spirit uses the word *parresia* in this verse to urge us to come "boldly" before God's throne of grace. This means that not only does Jesus beckon us to come to Him, but He also invites us to be *straight-to-the-point* when we talk to Him!

You need never fear that you are *too frank*, *too bold*, *too forthright*, *too honest*, *too outspoken*, or *too blunt* when you open your heart to God about your needs and struggles or when you request His help. Of course, you should never be irreverent — but neither do you need to be afraid to speak exactly what is on your heart. The Greek word *parresia* emphatically tells you that Jesus will never be turned off, offended, or insulted when you freely speak your heart and mind to Him. He *wants* to hear what you have to say!

Hebrews 4:16 goes on to tell us to "...come boldly unto the throne of grace, that we may *obtain* mercy, and find grace to help in time of need." The word "obtain" is from the Greek word *lambano* — a word that means *to seize* or *to lay hold of something in order to make it your very own*. It is the picture of reaching out *to grab*, *to capture*, or *to take possession* of something. Depending on the context in which it is used, *lambano* can either mean *to violently lay hold of something to seize and take it as one's very own*, or it can depict a person who *gently and graciously receives something that is freely and easily given*.

Jesus is always there, waiting mercifully to help anyone who comes to Him by faith. But your own personal circumstances or inward struggles could affect the ease with which you receive His help. If your struggle is intense, if your mind is tortured, if your flesh resists you, or if it seems like the world is pressing against you, you may find it difficult to freely receive from the Lord. In those moments, you have to reach out and *forcibly lay hold* of the help God offers you.

Jesus is ready and willing to simply give you what you need. All you have to do is open your heart and by faith *receive* it. Shove those negative circumstances and emotions out of the way, and reach out by faith to *lay hold of* the grace and mercy that Jesus so freely offers. It's time for you to *receive* the mercy He wants to give — but don't stop with mercy! If you'll keep pressing forward by faith, this verse promises that you will also "...find grace to help in time of need."

The word "find" is a translation of the Greek word *eurisko*, which means *to find*. It denotes *a discovery made by searching or by happenstance*. It usually denotes a discovery made as a result of an intense investigation, scientific study, or scholarly research. After working long hours and searching for a long time, the researcher suddenly finds what he has been seeking. In that unforgettable moment of joyful euphoria, he shrieks, "EUREKA!" — which means, "I FOUND IT!" The word *eureka* is derived from this Greek word *eurisko*, which lets us know the kind of intense joy that a person experiences when he finds the help for which he has sought for so long.

Praise God for those special times when a believer "happens" upon the help of God. I'm especially talking about times when someone is young in the Lord or when a person is too inexperienced to know what he's doing or even how to properly pray. Or perhaps a believer is innocently making all kinds of mistakes. Then somehow God's mercy and grace overrides all his blunders, and that precious believer is divinely and supernaturally plugged into help that causes him to rise above his circumstances and overcome every obstacle. That believer can't even explain what happened or how he received that divine assistance. All he knows is that suddenly he was *empowered*! In that moment, he "found" the help he needed to overcome what he was facing in life.

However, "help" doesn't usually come by happenstance; rather, it comes when a person diligently seeks the help he needs. When that diligent seeker lays hold of his answer from Heaven, such euphoria floods his heart that he exclaims, "I HAVE IT!"; "I'VE FOUND IT!"; or "I'VE RECEIVED IT!" At long last, the seeker is holding in his hand the answer he needed from God!

But I must point out one more very important thing about the word *eurisko*. This word can also be used to picture *someone who diligently seeks and therefore acquires something for someone else*. This has *powerful* connotations, and I want to tell you why.

It means you can go to Jesus, the Great High Priest, to obtain mercy and find help for others about whom you are worried or burdened. You can obtain help:

1. For those who need healing for their bodies.

2. For those who are bound and need deliverance.

3. For those who are tormented and need peace.

4. For marriages and families that are in trouble.

5. For provision to be given to those who need a financial break-through.

6. For those who are in need in any area of their lives.

Not only can you take your own needs to Jesus, but you can also take *others'* needs to Jesus and obtain the help *they* so desperately need.

Now let's look at the phrase "help in time of need," which is a translation of the word *boetheia*, a word that primarily had a military connotation. It can simply be translated to *help* meet someone's needs. But when you understand the military implications of this word, it becomes *truly* powerful.

The word *boetheia* was first and foremost used to describe that moment when a soldier got into trouble. When his fellow soldiers were alerted to his dangerous situation, they were completely dedicated to the goal of going into battle to defend their co-fighter and fighting for his well-being, safety, and security. Just hearing that a fellow soldier was in need was enough to beckon the other soldiers into battle and motivate them to spare no effort in order to rescue him and bring him back to a place of safety and protection.

Because *boetheia* is the word used in this text, we know that when we get into trouble and Jesus hears about it, He will come to our defense! He will do battle for us in our time of need. If we will go to Jesus, our Great High Priest, and present our case to Him, He will intercede for us — rising up like a Mighty Warrior who is ready to go into battle to fight for us until we are delivered and free. That is the "help" we will find when we present our needs to Jesus.

Think about it: Why would we ever try to fight our battles alone when the Greatest Warrior in the universe — the One who possesses ultimate power — is willing to fight for us?

So, then, what is the answer to the question: "Where is Jesus, and what has He been doing for the past 2,000 years?"

After Jesus' work on the Cross was finished and He was raised from the dead, He ascended on High and sat down at the Father's right hand. Today Jesus ever lives to make intercession for you and for anyone who comes to Him by faith. He fights for every believer who comes boldly and honestly to Him and who earnestly seeks His assistance. I would say that this ministry has kept Jesus pretty busy for the past 2,000 years!

Why would Jesus come to earth, humble Himself to the point of dying on the Cross, be raised from the dead, and pour out the gift of the Holy Spirit to empower you — only to then reject or resist you when you come to Him with your needs? He wouldn't! Because He was obedient, even unto death on a Cross, Jesus was highly exalted above all other names, whether in Heaven, on earth, or under the earth (Philippians 2:8-10). And from His highly exalted place, He still has His eyes fixed on *you*.

Nearly 2,000 years ago, Jesus died for you. But today — right at this very moment — He lives to intercede for you and to fight for your every need.

Think About It

Jesus conquered death, hell, and the grave, and now He lives forever to make intercession for you! Meditate on this truth: The Creator of the Universe came to earth to experience everything you could ever go through. He paid the penalty for every sin you would ever commit. And now He is seated beside the Father in Heaven, speaking on your behalf.

You have a representative in Heaven who has already faced every temptation you'll ever face and has endured every pain you've ever experienced. He completely identifies with your human condition. When you come boldly before Him with your petitions, Jesus is able and willing to save you or others to the uttermost. No matter what situation you may be facing, God is for you, *not* against you. Think about *that*!

God likes straight talk. People may feel challenged by direct, confident communication, but God expects it. Irreverence is inappropriate, of course, but honesty is what God wants when you pour out your heart to Him. But you can't be honest with God or confident in His presence until you're willing to be honest with yourself.

Perhaps you've been praying and even worrying about a situation for some time. Have you searched your own heart to be certain you're telling yourself the truth about the matter without excuses or denial? Think about it. The Person of the Holy Spirit is the Spirit of Truth. He will help you press past your own inner struggles to know and understand truth so you can move forward and go before God in confidence. Ask Him.

The ministry of the Holy Spirit is to help you do the will of God, just as He empowered Jesus to do God's will during Jesus' earthly ministry. Every frailty and insufficiency of the human condition is counteracted by the wisdom and all-sufficiency of the Holy Spirit. He will lead and guide you into all truth and show you things to come. And by the strength of His might within you, the Holy Spirit will enable you to do whatever the will of God requires of you.

Think about the specific areas in your life and the different ways in which you need to ask for and yield to the help of the Holy Spirit.

chapter

35

Copy Every Stroke of the Master

chapter

35

Copy Every Stroke of the Master

For even hereunto were ye called:
because Christ suffered for us, leaving us an example,
that ye should follow in his steps.
— 1 Peter 2:21

Now that you've walked with Jesus through His most trying moments during His final hours on earth, you should know that the Holy Spirit is waiting to walk with you through *your* most trying experiences. The same Spirit who raised Jesus from the dead wants to give you the wisdom you need and to strengthen your spirit, soul, and body for whatever you must face along the way in your own journey through life.

So what's the next step? When it's time to put down this book and face the challenges of the coming days, how do you effectively apply what you've learned about Jesus to your own life?

Let me begin to answer those questions by taking you back for a moment to my first-grade classroom. How well I remember learning to write in the first grade! I carefully studied how my teacher wrote the letters of the alphabet on the blackboard. When she was done, it was our turn to take our lead pencils in hand to copy what she'd written.

With all my might, I'd press down with my pencil onto the paper of my Indian Chief tablet. I pushed so hard writing those letters that I formed a callous on my finger I still have to this day! I gave 100 percent of my concentration to exactly duplicating every letter my teacher had written on that blackboard. Day after day, I'd write those letters over and over and over again, filling my tablet with pages of writing until I finally mastered each letter of the alphabet. It took concentration and commitment, but in time I learned to write those letters exactly as my teacher had shown me.

I'm sure you, too, can remember when you first learned to write. But did you know that this is precisely the idea the apostle Peter had in mind when he told the early believers, "For even hereunto were ye called: because Christ suffered for us, leaving us an example, that we should follow in his steps" (1 Peter 2:21)? Let me explain what I mean.

When Peter wrote these words to early believers, they were suffering terribly for their faith at the hands of the Roman government. For them, there was no legal recourse. They were suffering unjustly, and there was nothing they could do legally to defend themselves. God's Word commanded them to respect, submit to, and pray for the very government that was harassing and killing them. To the believers who were facing this plight of unjust treatment, Peter said this: "For even hereunto were ye called: because Christ suffered for us, leaving us an example, that ye should follow in his steps" (1 Peter 2:21).

The word "suffered" in this verse comes from the Greek word *pascho*, meaning *to suffer*. It's the word used to describe the *passion* or *suffering* of Jesus when He died on the Cross. You now have a deeper sense of all that this word entails after reading in earlier chapters about Jesus' suffering in His final hours. However, there are many other examples of the word *pascho* in the New Testament, and they all carry the idea of *suffering, undergoing hardship, being ill-treated,* or *experiencing adversity.*

The truth is, Jesus experienced a measure of suffering throughout His entire life on this earth. When He was a child, His family suffered as they fled from the murderous plots of King Herod. Later Jesus suffered at the hands of religious leaders who hated Him and continually leveled false accusations against Him. Jesus had to constantly put up with the immature behavior of His disciples as He tried to teach them and set an example for them.

Then as we have seen, Jesus suffered betrayal at the hands of one of His associates, Judas Iscariot. His suffering in the Garden of Gethsemane was so intense that His sweat was as great drops of blood falling down to the ground. And in the end, Jesus suffered the worst suffering of all — death on the Cross. Yet through it all, Jesus lived above the suffering and maintained an attitude of love toward those who treated Him unjustly.

Peter reminded his readers of Jesus' suffering, hardship, and ill treatment in order to draw the early believers closer to the Lord in the midst of what they were experiencing themselves. At that time, they desperately needed to know how to respond to unjust situations they could not change. Since no one was better at dealing with such challenges than Jesus, Peter reminded his readers (and us) that "…Christ suffered for us, leaving us an *example*…."

Now we return to the picture of a child learning to write the letters of the alphabet. When Peter chose to use the word "example" in this verse, he reached into the world of early education and borrowed the word *hupogrammos*. This is a word that paints a picture of a schoolchild who carefully watches his teacher write the letters of the alphabet. Then that child painstakingly copies each letter, matching it as closely as possible to the original letters written by his teacher.

If you remember your childhood as well as I remember mine, I'm sure it isn't too hard for you to remember straining to see exactly how the teacher wrote each letter and then trying to copy every stroke. You leaned over your desk, pressing down on your tablet with your pencil, focusing intensely on copying each letter perfectly.

This is exactly the picture Peter has in mind when he tells you to follow the "example" of Jesus. Since Jesus is your Teacher and Master, you must focus on your spiritual blackboard — the Word of God — to learn from Him and then reproduce His example in your own life.

You must learn:

- ❖ How the Master dealt with unfair criticism so you can respond like Him when you are unfairly criticized.

- ❖ How Jesus responded to attacks that were waged against Him so you can know how to respond in His strength to attacks that come against you.

- ❖ How Jesus responded to people when they failed or betrayed Him so you can respond the same way when people disappoint or hurt you.

- ❖ How Jesus carried Himself with grace and dignity even in the midst of unspeakable abuse, so you can then draw on His strength to walk through difficult situations with the same grace and dignity.

- ❖ How He forgave His accusers every step of the way so you can freely forgive those who mistreat or malign you.

You cannot avoid the fact that you will sometimes face unpleasant situations in which you feel mistreated, abused, or discriminated against. As long as you live in a world where the devil operates and unsaved people have their way, evil and injustice will touch your life from time to time. So when you find yourself subjected to a situation that seems unfair and unjust, you must ask, *How does God expect me to respond?*

Of course, you should pray for God to change a difficult situation. Prayer can make a huge difference in any circumstance. But what if the situation doesn't change as quickly as you wish? How should you respond? For example:

- ❖ If your employer treats you badly for no obvious reason and the situation goes on for a long time, what should you do? Of course, you could go find another job. But what if you *know* that your current job is where God wants you and that you're not to leave it? How should you respond to the foul treatment you are receiving from your superior?

❖ If fellow employees are out to hurt you, to undercut you, or to see you demoted, what course of action should you take? Perhaps you've taken steps to befriend them, but nothing seems to improve the situation. How should you respond to the unfair treatment you're experiencing?

❖ Maybe you feel persecuted by fellow students who don't share your faith in Christ and who dislike your personal convictions. You know you can't quit school as a reaction to this difficult situation. But exactly how *does* God expect you to respond?

❖ Perhaps your family members are hostile to you because they don't understand your faith or they don't agree with the direction you're taking in life. How should you respond to your loved ones? It's so very important that you know how to respond when your family doesn't agree or support what you are doing — especially when you *know* the Holy Spirit is the One leading you to take that course of direction.

Certainly you must do everything possible to resolve conflicts with friends and family and to protect yourself and your reputation spiritually and legally. Yet sometimes things happen that are beyond your control, that are not so easily resolved, and for which there is no easy recourse. Whenever you're feeling maligned and mistreated, remember that it's a prime opportunity for the devil to tempt you to become bitter, angry, hard-hearted, and resentful of those who have treated you unjustly. If you yield to that temptation, your wrong response won't do anything to improve your situation, but it *will* produce negative consequences in your own life.

That's why you must absolutely refuse to allow the devil to sow into your heart those negative emotions that bear only bad fruit. Harboring such emotions is *never* the answer, no matter what situation you might be facing in life. Having read the preceding chapters, you already know that to be true.

I believe you've gained new insight into Jesus' journey of pain, betrayal, and disappointment that consumed His final hours. Now I encourage you to take some time to consider His great love for you and the power He has made available to you by laying down His own life that you might know eternal life. Perhaps in a deeper way than you've ever done before, invite Jesus to walk with you through your own journey, guiding you by His Spirit through each difficulty and challenge that arises along the way.

It's very important that you know *exactly* how God expects you to respond when you find yourself in a difficult predicament you have no ability to change — and there's no better example to emulate than Jesus. So go to the Gospels and begin to read those pages with the heart of a student who studies and endeavors to copy every stroke of his teacher's pen. Seek to extract truth and specific answers for your life and the situations you're facing right now. Observe how Jesus conducted Himself in similar circumstances. Then like a child learning to write, make your best effort to copy each stroke of the Master.

You probably won't get it exactly right the first time, but don't give up. Just like the student who is learning to write, you must commit yourself to try and try again until you have finally mastered each stroke and have learned to successfully respond to difficult situations as Jesus did when He walked the earth.

Perhaps you've been praying for guidance, trying to understand how to deal with the conflicts you've encountered. Now you know that the answers you need are found in the life of Jesus. He is your Chief Example, your Teacher, your Master — the One you are called to copy. So in addition to praying for wisdom and guidance, it's time for you to open your Bible and start reading all four Gospels to see what Jesus did in the same kind of situations you're facing. Learn from the life of the Master, and walk through your situation in the same manner Jesus walked through His most difficult challenges.

As we've seen, no one was ever more mistreated than Jesus. Yet when soldiers spat on Him, when Pilate ordered Him to be scourged, when religious leaders laughed at Him, and even when He was betrayed by one of His own disciples — Jesus continued to walk in love, forgiving them all. He is our Example, showing us how we should respond when we face injustice, when someone offends or hurts us, or when we find ourselves in difficult circumstances beyond our control.

Learn from the life of the Master, and walk through your situation in the same manner Jesus walked through His most difficult challenges.

Are you facing difficult times? Are you being accused of things you didn't do or blamed for things of which you have no knowledge? Are you being mistreated or discriminated against? If you answered yes to any of these questions, this is the moment for you to turn your eyes to the blackboard — God's Word — and study each stroke of the Master. Once you see what He did and how He responded in situations similar to yours, it is then your task to copy Him. If you'll take this approach to the challenges you're facing right now that seem so distressing, you'll begin to see those situations as opportunities to become more like Jesus.

So make it your earnest goal to apply to your own life the principles of Jesus' life —especially the truths and principles revealed in what He experienced in His final days on earth. Strive to pen the strokes of your moments on this earth to reflect each stroke of the Master.

If you will let the Holy Spirit help you, it is possible for you to successfully walk through life as Jesus did. What a blessing that you don't have to figure it all out by yourself! Just study the strokes of the Master's pen, and press forward by faith to copy those strokes in the face of every challenge that arises.

By yourself, you cannot do it. But Jesus didn't leave you to face the challenges of life alone and without help. After purchasing the full price of your redemption, He ascended on High, where He now intercedes continually before the Father on your behalf (Hebrews 7:25). And just as He promised, Jesus sent the Holy Spirit to dwell within you as your Teacher and Guide and to fill and empower you so you can walk as Jesus walked through every situation you could ever face.

Jesus did the hard part. All that He suffered, He suffered for you, leaving behind a perfect example for you to follow. As you respond with His wisdom and love in the face of every challenge, light *will* overcome darkness and God's purposes *will* be fulfilled. Victory will always be the outcome when, by God's grace and the help of His Spirit, you learn to copy the strokes of the Master.

*Isn't It Time To Make
a Change in Your Life?*

Isn't It Time To Make a Change in Your Life?

From Gethsemane's garden to Golgotha's hill, Jesus Christ experienced the full spectrum of emotional and physical anguish — more than any other human would ever endure. Such suffering was the penalty of sin, or of the willful disconnection from God, and Jesus accepted it by choice. Decreed by God before Adam chose treason, death was the ultimate payment for sin. The holiness and justice of God required sin's penalty to be paid. But God's love and devotion for man prompted Him to mercifully provide a substitute.

Initially, God allowed the blood of animals to provide a covering for sin. But only a Man with sinless blood could provide cleansing for sin, paying the ultimate price by offering His life as payment in full for the judgment against mankind. Thus, Jesus Christ — God in the form of a perfect Man — came to take away the sins of the world. Jesus died to pay the ultimate price once and for all and to break the power of sin. Then He rose triumphant over death, hell, and the grave to provide enduring freedom from sin and its destructive consequences.

What does this mean for you today, 2,000 years after Christ's death and resurrection? It means that Jesus gained total victory over sin and wickedness so you can walk in that same victory too.

So how does that victory look on a daily basis?

Consider what you've just learned about Jesus — not merely what He went through, but the way He responded as He went through it. Nothing about His attitude or actions reflected weakness or fear. Even when enduring excruciating pain and humiliation, even when facing the most horrendous form of death, Jesus was at all times in complete control of

His emotions and His words as He drew His strength from His Heavenly Father.

When Jesus was surrounded by liars who unjustly accused Him and called for His death, He didn't wither and collapse emotionally, nor did He try to beg or negotiate His way out of the situation. He knew who He was and what He had come to do, and He held fast to His trust in His Father. Jesus knew that His life was in God's hands, not man's.

So it is with you. Remember that when you feel overwhelmed and surrounded by adversity or opposition. Remember the strength Jesus walked in, and choose to draw upon that strength every day of your life. If you are a child of God, the same Spirit who raised Jesus from the dead dwells in *you*. The Holy Spirit will not only raise you to a newness of life, but He will also raise up God's purposes for your life that may seem dead to you now. Because your debt is paid in full, you can tap into resurrection life and move forward in the face of blistering betrayal or opposition on any level.

If sickness or disease attempts to latch onto you, remember the stripes Jesus bore to obtain healing and wholeness for you. If pain grips your body or if a report of disease threatens to rob your peace of mind, crowd you with fear, and shorten your life, remember Jesus. Remember how the cruel Roman lash lacerated His holy body, ripping into His flesh, gouging Him repeatedly until the blood flowed unrestrained. Remember that He was wounded for *your* transgressions and bruised for *your* iniquities. The chastisement that was needed to obtain *your* peace of mind was laid on Him. And by the stripes that wounded Jesus, *you* were healed.

From this moment forward, your life can be different than it's ever been before because your debt of sin has been *paid in full* by Jesus Christ.

Prayer of Salvation

When Jesus Christ comes into your life, you are immediately emancipated — totally set free from the bondage of sin!

If you have never received Jesus as your personal Savior, it is time to experience this new life for yourself! The first step to freedom is simple. Just pray this prayer from your heart:

Lord, I can never adequately thank You for all You did for me on the Cross. I am so undeserving, Jesus, but You came and gave Your life for me anyway. I repent and turn from my sins right now, Jesus. I receive You as my Savior, and I ask You to wash away my sin by Your precious blood. I thank You from the depths of my heart for doing what no one else could do for me. Had it not been for Your willingness to lay down Your life for me, I would be eternally lost.

Thank You, Jesus, that I am now redeemed by Your blood. You bore my sin, my sickness, my pain, my lack of peace, and my suffering on the Cross. Your blood has cleansed me from my sin and washed me whiter than snow, giving me rightstanding with the Father. I have no need to be ashamed of my past sins, because I am now a new creature in You. Old things have passed away, and all things have become new because I am in Jesus Christ (1 Corinthians 5:17).

Because of You, Jesus, today I am forgiven; I am filled with peace; and I am a joint heir with You! Satan no longer has a right to lay any claim on me. From a grateful heart, I will faithfully serve You the rest of my days!

If you prayed this prayer from your heart, something amazing has happened to you. No longer a servant to sin, you are now a servant of Almighty God. The evil spirits that once exacted every ounce of your being and required your all-inclusive servitude no longer possess the authorization to control you or to dictate your destiny.

As a result of your decision to turn your life over to Jesus Christ, your eternal home has been decided forever. HEAVEN is now your permanent address.

God's Spirit has moved into your own human spirit, and you have become the "temple of God" (1 Corinthians 6:19). What a miracle! To think that God, by His Spirit, now lives inside of you! I have never ceased to be amazed at this incredible miracle of God in my own life. He gave me (and you!) a new heart and then made us His home!

Now you have a new Lord and Master, and His name is Jesus. From this moment on, the Spirit of God will work in you and supernaturally energize you to fulfill God's will for your life. Everything will change for you now — and it's all going to change for the best!

Prayer of Forgiveness

No one is spared opportunities for offense in this life. Not one person escapes times of dealing with disappointment and hurt as the result of other people's words or actions. But how one *responds* to hurt, betrayal, or offense makes all the difference in the outcome — in the lives of both the offender and the one offended.

In this matter of forgiveness, you are called to follow the example of Jesus, for the Bible declares that "...as He is, so are we in this world" (1 John 4:17). Jesus walked the path of forgiveness in the face of unspeakable horrors committed against Him during His final hours on this earth. In light of His example, can you do any less than release in forgiveness those who have hurt or offended you?

Take the time to pray this prayer from your heart:

Dear Heavenly Father,

I thank You for the great love You expressed when You sent Jesus to be my Savior, my Substitute, and my Example. As I look at Jesus' life and His responses to all that He experienced, I see Your heart and mind revealed. Thank You, Father, for loving me so completely and for forgiving me so fully.

Right now, Father, I come before You as humbly and as sincerely as I know how to honor You for the great sacrifice of Your Son. I honor You by acknowledging and receiving the power of the blood that Jesus so willingly shed for the forgiveness and removal of my sins. And just as I require and receive the power of that precious blood in my life, I release its cleansing power in forgiveness toward those who have hurt or wronged me in the past.

Father, as an act of my will, I choose to believe and act upon Your Word that tells me to forgive. I know You said that great peace belongs to those who love Your law and that nothing shall offend them (Psalm 119:165). I feel the sting of betrayal, but I'm not ignorant of the enemy's devices. The purpose of betrayal is to produce a root of bitterness in me, and I refuse to yield to that sin. Father, I forgive — and I ask You to forgive those who have hurt me, too, for they don't know what they're doing. They don't realize that what has been said and done against me has been said and done against You. Forgive them, Father.

Holy Spirit, I ask You to help me yield to the love of God that has already been shed abroad in my heart by Your presence within me. As You strengthened Jesus, please strengthen me. Help me walk in the love, the Word, and the will of God toward those who have wronged me. Help me respond just as Jesus responded when He was spitefully treated and wrongfully accused. I take comfort and find strength in Jesus' example before me and in Your mighty presence within me, Holy Spirit. Help me lean upon You without reservation and to respond to You without hesitation. And help those I have forgiven to turn their hearts toward You. May we both embrace Your wisdom and Your ways so that Your purpose may be fulfilled in each of our lives.

Thank You, Father, for the blood that has the power to cleanse sin and to remove barriers. I ask that You intervene in our hearts and in this situation to turn all that the enemy meant for evil toward our good and Your glory. I receive this as done in Jesus' name. Amen.

Prayer for Healing

Jesus purchased complete redemption for you. Through the sacrifice of His life and the spilling of His blood, He paid the full price for your freedom from sin *and* sickness.

With every stroke of the vicious Roman whip He suffered, Jesus bore the penalty of your physical pains, sicknesses, and diseases. Today Heaven declares that "…by whose [Jesus'] stripes, you *were* healed" (1 Peter 2:24). The price has been paid in full for you to receive the gift of divine health though Jesus Christ. Receive by faith complete healing for your body as you pray this prayer.

Dear Heavenly Father,

Jesus endured the horrors of the Roman scourge to pay the penalty for my sin. Before Jesus ever stood in that place, You declared through Isaiah that His suffering secured my deliverance and by the stripes that wounded Him, I was healed (Isaiah 53:5).

Jesus, the Lamb of God, justified many — and through the sacrifice of Himself, my debt was paid in full. Therefore, I come boldly before Your throne of grace to receive the help and healing I need.

I thank You, Father, that it pleased You to lay my sickness, infirmity, and disease upon Jesus so that I might receive health and healing in exchange. Right now I behold the Lamb, who was slain to set me free. And I receive freedom — the freedom He died and rose again to purchase for me — from sin, sickness, and disease. With every torturous lash of the whip and every mutilating gash it produced, Jesus purchased my healing with His own blood.

Today, Father, I come before You to receive the healing Jesus purchased for me. Just as my salvation is based on Jesus and His completed work, so is my healing. I don't have to beg You for it. I simply receive. And as I receive Your great gift of healing, I honor Your Son's great sacrifice that opened the door for me to receive Your life-giving power to meet my every need. For this and for all You've done for me, I thank You, Father, in Jesus' name. Amen.

Endnotes

CHAPTER 5

[1] For a detailed account of the Tower of Antonia, *see:*
Antiquities
Flavius Josephus
Book XV, Chapter 11, Paragraph 4

CHAPTER 14

[2] *Antiquities*
Flavius Josephus
Book XVIII, Chapter 2, Paragraph 2

[3] *War of the Jews*
Flavius Josephus
Book II, Chapter 8, Paragraph 14

CHAPTER 17

[4] *Antiquities*
Flavius Josephus
Book XVIII, Chapter 4, Paragraph 2

CHAPTER 19

[5] *See* Josephus for an in-depth examination of all the members of the Herodian family.

CHAPTER 22

[6] Edwards, Gobles, and Hosmer, 1986.
"On the Physical Death of Jesus Christ"
JAMA 255:1455-1463

[7] *Church History*
Eusebius
Book IV, Chapter 11

CHAPTER 24

[8] *Antiquities*
Flavius Josephus
Book XVIII, Chapter 4, Paragraph 2

CHAPTER 25

[9] *War of the Jews*
Flavius Josephus
Book V, Chapter 11, Paragraph 1

CHAPTER 27

[10] *Chronicle*, Olympiad, trans. Carrier (1999). Eusebius quotes Phelgon.

[11] *Against Celsus*
Origen
Chapter XXXIII

Greek and English
New Testament Study Helps
Reference Book List

1. *How To Use New Testament Greek Study Aids* by Walter Jerry Clark (Loizeaux Brothers).

2. *Strong's Exhaustive Concordance of the Bible* by James H. Strong.

3. *The Interlinear Greek-English New Testament* by George Ricker Berry (Baker Book House).

4. *The Englishman's Greek Concordance of the New Testament* by George Wigram (Hendrickson).

5. *New Thayer's Greek-English Lexicon of the New Testament* by Joseph Thayer (Hendrickson).

6. *The Expanded Vine's Expository Dictionary of New Testament Words* by W. E. Vine (Bethany).

7. *New International Dictionary of New Testament Theology (DNTT);* Colin Brown, editor (Zondervan).

8. *Theological Dictionary of the New Testament (TDNT)* by Geoffrey Bromiley; Gephard Kittle, editor (Eerdmans Publishing Co.).

9. *The New Analytical Greek Lexicon;* Wesley Perschbacher, editor (Hendrickson).

10. *The Linguistic Key to the Greek New Testament* by Fritz Rienecker and Cleon Rogers (Zondervan).

11. *Word Studies in the Greek New Testament* by Kenneth Wuest, 4 Volumes (Eerdmans).

12. *New Testament Words* by William Barclay (Westminster Press).

13. *Antiquities by* Flavius Josephus.

14. *War of the Jews* by Flavius Josephus.
15. *Church History* by Eusebius.
16. *Against Celsus* by Origen.

About the Author

Rick Renner is a highly respected leader and teacher within the Christian community, both in the U.S. and abroad. He fills a unique position in the modern Christian world, combining an extraordinary depth of scriptural and practical knowledge with an easy-to-understand, faith-filled approach to the Bible. Many internationally renowned Christian leaders seek out his insight on doctrine, theology, and practical application.

Rick works alongside his wife Denise to see the Gospel preached, leadership trained, and the churches established throughout the world. Rick's broadcast "Good News With Rick Renner" can be seen across the entire former USSR. He has distributed hundreds of thousands of teaching audio and videotapes, and his best-selling books have been translated into four major languages.

Rick is the founder of the *"It's Possible"* humanitarian foundation, an organization committed to providing for the practical needs of various segments of Russian society. Rick is also the founder of the *Good News Association of Pastors and Churches*, through which he oversees and strengthens hundreds of churches throughout the former Soviet Union. In addition, Rick and Denise pastor the thriving *Moscow Good News Church*, located in the very heart of Moscow, Russia, as well as the rapidly growing *Kiev Good News Church* in the capital city of Ukraine.

About Our Work
in the Former USSR

Since 1991 when God first called Rick and Denise Renner to the former Soviet Union, millions of lives have been touched by the various outreaches of *Rick Renner Ministries*. Nevertheless, the Renners' ever-increasing vision for this region of the world continues to expand across 11 time zones to reach 300 million precious lives for God's Kingdom.

The *Moscow Good News Church* was begun in September 2000 in the very heart of Moscow, right next to Red Square. Since that time, the church has grown to become one of the largest Protestant churches in Moscow and a strategic model for pastors throughout this region of the world to learn from and emulate. Today the outreaches of the *Moscow Good News Church* includes ministry to families, senior citizens, children, youth, and international church members, as well as a specialized ministry to businesspeople and an outreach to the poor and needy. The Renners simultaneously pastor the *Kiev Good News Church*, located in Kiev, Ukraine, another part of their ongoing vision to reach the former Soviet Union with the Gospel of Jesus Christ.

Part of the mission of *Rick Renner Ministries* is to come alongside pastors and ministers and take them to a higher level of excellence and professionalism in the ministry. Therefore, since 1991 when the walls of communism first collapsed, this ministry has been working in the former USSR to train and equip pastors, church leaders, and ministers, helping them attain the necessary skills and knowledge to fulfill the ministries that the Lord has given to them.

To this end, Rick Renner founded both a seminary and a ministerial association. The *Good News Seminary* is a school that operates as a part of the *Moscow Good News Church*. It specializes in training leaders to start new churches all over the former USSR. The *Good News Association of Pastors and Churches* is a church-planting and church-supporting organization with a membership of pastors and churches that numbers in the hundreds.

Rick Renner Ministries also owns and operates the *Good News Television Network*, the first and one of the largest TV outreaches within the territory of the former USSR. Since its inception in 1992, this television network has become one of the strongest instruments available today for declaring the Word of God to the 15 nations of the former Soviet Union, reaching 110 million potential viewers every day with the Gospel of Jesus Christ.

In addition, Rick Renner also founded the *"It's Possible!"* humanitarian foundation, which is involved in various outreaches in the city of Moscow. The *"It's Possible"* foundation uses innovative methods to help different age groups of people who are in great need. For example, the *"It's Possible"* humanitarian foundation provides quality entertainment and distributes literature and vitamins to thousands of elderly people.

If you would like to learn more about our work in the former Soviet Union, please visit our website at www.renner.org, or call 918-496-3213.

For Further Information

For all book orders, please contact:

Teach All Nations

A book company anointed to take God's Word
to you and to the nations of the world.

A Division of
Rick Renner Ministries
P.O. Box 702040
Tulsa, OK 74170-2040
Phone: 877-281-8644
FAx: 918-496-3278
E-mail: tan@renner.org

*For prayer requests
or for further information about this ministry,
please write or call the Rick Renner Ministries office
nearest you (see following page).*

FREE PRODUCT CATALOG

To order a complete audio, video, and book catalog, please contact our office in Tulsa.

Rick Renner Ministries

www.renner.org

All USA Correspondence:
Rick Renner Ministries
P. O. Box 702040
Tulsa, OK 74170-2040
(918) 496-3213
Or 1-800-RICK-593
E-mail: renner@renner.org
Website: www.renner.org

Riga Office:
Rick Renner Ministries
Unijas 99
Riga, LV-1084, Latvia
(371) 780-2150
E-mail: info@goodnews.lv

Moscow Office:
Rick Renner Ministries
P. O. Box 53
Moscow, 109316, Russia
7 (095) 727-1470
E-mail: mirpress@umail.ru
Website: www.mgnc.org

Kiev Office:
Rick Renner Ministries
P. O. Box 146
Kiev, 01025, Ukraine
380 (44) 246-6552
E-mail: mirpress@rrm.kiev.ua

Oxford Office:
Rick Renner Ministries
Box 7, 266 Banbury Road
Oxford, OX2 7DL, England
E-mail: europe@renner.org

A Biblical Approach to Spiritual Warfare

Rick Renner's book *Dressed To Kill* is considered by many to be a true classic on the subject of scriptural warfare. The original version, which sold more than 400,000 copies, is a curriculum staple in Bible schools worldwide. In this beautifully bound hardback volume, you will find:

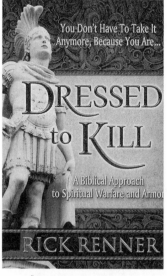

- 512 pages of reedited text
- 16 pages of full-color illustrations
- Questions at the end of each chapter to guide you into deeper study

In *Dressed To Kill*, Rick explains with exacting detail the purpose and function of each piece of Roman armor. In the process, he describes the signifi-

$24.95 (Hardback)
ISBN: 978-0-9779459-0-0

cance of our *spiritual* armor not only to withstand the onslaughts of the enemy and but also to overturn the tendencies of the carnal mind. Furthermore, Rick delivers a clear, scriptural presentation on the biblical definition of spiritual warfare — what it is and what it is not.

When you walk with God in deliberate, continual fellowship, He will enrobe you with Himself. Armed with the knowledge of who you are in Him, you will be dressed and dangerous to the works of darkness, unflinching in the face of conflict, and fully equipped to take the offensive and gain mastery over any opposition from your spiritual foe. You don't have to accept defeat anymore once you are *dressed to kill*!

Books by Rick Renner

Books in English and Russian
Seducing Spirits and Doctrines of Demons
Living in the Combat Zone
Merchandising the Anointing
Dressed To Kill
Spiritual Weapons To Defeat the Enemy
Dream Thieves
The Point of No Return
The Dynamic Duo
If You Were God, Would You Choose You?
Ten Guidelines To Help You Achieve Your Long-Awaited
  PROMOTION!
It's Time for You To Fulfill Your Secret Dreams
Isn't It Time for You To Get Over It?
Sparkling Gems From the Greek Daily Devotional
Insights to Successful Leadership

Books in Russian Only
Hell Is a Real Place
What the Bible Says About Water Baptism
What the Bible Says About Healing
What the Bible Says About Tithes and Offerings
How To Test Spiritual Manifestations
Good News About Your New Life
What To Do if You've Had a Failure

Study Notes

Study Notes

Study Notes